NUT JOB

A.J. SCHMITZ

MAXIXAM
PRESS

For mom and dad.

Remember when I fell off that hayride?

Other books by A.J. Schmitz you've neglected:

Buggin' Out

The Death of Our Dreams: And Other Funny Stories

Dear Norman

Everything in this book is true.

Some of the names have been changed
to protect the guilty, the innocent, and other mumbo jumbo
I felt I should put in here so I don't get sued.

CONTENTS

New York State of Mind

New Yorkers are in such a rush. Where are they going? Can anyone stop them long enough to ask? They're screaming by like they've been shot out of a cannon. Humming along like bees.

"I wanna donut before the line is too long!"

"I have a meeting!"

"I need coffee!"

Their feet are on fire – smoke billowing off their rubber soles. They're cranking along like those Olympic speed-walkers. You've seen them -- hips swinging and arms pumping like pistons. They're flying. Like someone pushed them down a flight of varnished stairs in slippers made of ice.

"Excuse me."

"Coming through!"

The city sidewalks are flowing like veins. Like adrenaline pushing through at warp speed. Don't stop short or you'll get run over. Cause a logjam… a clot. Slow down to contemplate a sandwich on 3rd avenue and you'll cause a delay on 5th avenue. The sidewalk is a pedestrian highway. Need to go the other way? Pull over and think about it. Then merge into traffic – hang a U-ey.

Take a bad step and you'll get a face full of chest... a mouth full of coat buttons.

People think New Yorkers are rude, but they're just in a rush. Hustling. Bustling. Running everywhere. They're absolute nut jobs! But, they see a confused tourist with a map and they grind to a halt.

They must help!

They surround a foreign couple like an intervention. They get their fellow New Yorkers involved.

"Where you from? The Bronx? You're our northern connection."

"What about you? Brooklyn? Southern connection!"

"Let's get these people where they need to go!!"

The foreign couple barely speak English but they know they're in good hands. They were lost, but now they're found.

"Where you going? Times square? Fuck it! I'll walk you there myself!"

"How fast can you walk?!"

"Let's go!"

Everyone's off like lightning. You have to be a trained athlete to keep up. Legs moving like a centipede. Sweat pouring off them like a marathoner.

The New York committee pool their information – working together in sweet harmony.

"The 6 train? No way! They'll be on that for hours. Take the Q or the R!"

"The R line is under construction! Take the green line for chrissakes!"

And they're off again like a 100-yard dash.

"You hungry?"

"There's an awesome Cuban place right around the corner!"

Before you know it, the foreign couple is fed, bathed and ready for a night on the town.

"You're welcome."

"Enjoy."

"See ya!"

The New York committee disperses like a crime scene. Gone as fast as they came. On to the next thing. On a mission. Everyone's in a different part of the city within minutes, bounding from one place to the next. The guy from Brooklyn is now in the Bronx. The guy from the Bronx is now in Miami.

"Sorry, gotta run!"

They're catching trains – catching flights. Catching colds. They're running with runny noses.

"I'm fine."

"I'll call you from the hospital."

They can't be ill. They got plans! There's agendas, calendars, itineraries and schedules.

"I'll call you from my cell phone."

"No, my other cell phone!"

It's impossible to go hungry in NYC. There's a place to eat every two feet. If you're too busy to enter a joint, hit a hot dog stand. The guy may nail your open palm with a foot-long while you're still moving. The nut girl too. She'll toss a steaming bag of chestnuts like a baseball pitcher. Exchange cash and go. There's no time to stop. Gotta keep pushing! Fruit guy too. He'll have the entire fruit section in a bag before you finish pointing at what you want.

"Banan…

"Here's your Bananas!"

"Thanks. Keep the change. Gotta keep truckin'!"

Pizza and bagels are good finger food. Eat on the run. Some countries eat pizza with a fork and knife. It's laughable. New Yorkers eat pizza on the go while yapping on the phone and splitting a fucking atom.

They're multi-tasking, Zen-master octopi.

"I'll be there in ten minutes"

But they're twenty minutes away! How is it possible? They'll shave the ten minutes off somewhere – somehow. They'll find the time. Erase the space. Hustle like maniacs. They'll *will it* into reality.

Cars are zooming around too. The pedestrian is king in New York.

"We're walking here!"

Don't step in the cross walk. Block the box. The light turns green and the gas pedals are STOMPED. They go one block and stop again. A child with six-inch legs can go faster than the average taxi. They're with their parents and the parents are *hauling ass*. They have to go. Daycare and work. They're running behind even though they're bookin' like sprinters. They could beat the 4-minute mile. Their Fitbits are chirping like songbirds as they crush every walking record imaginable.

"C'mon honey, we're late."

"Stop dragging"

"I've got a million things to do!"

They're making million dollar deals while leaping over gutters. Rainwater, garbage and the homeless can't stop them. These are small obstacles – mere child's play. Gotta keep moving!

"Put it on the Peterson account!"

"Don't ask questions!"

"This reservation was impossible!"

Gunshots won't deter them either. Just noise. They're wearing sound cancelling ear-buds. The music is chugging as they pound the pavement. Death metal, Hip Hop, Synthwave… the soundtracks of the city. The sound of energy. Throbbing beats. The music is pumping and so are their calves. They're burning fat, calories and their paychecks. New York is expensive. If you move fast enough you won't notice.

"Dinner at 9?"

"I'm 80 blocks away."

"I'll be there in 3 minutes."

Everything is around the corner, but there's a billion corners. Your corner may have something someone wants. They're flying to that corner – Uptown. You're going to their corner – downtown. We're all from a corner. Your corner of the world, their corner of the world. The four corners of the world. Brilliant corners. Square pegs in round holes.

New Yorkers live fast and love hard. They're looking for love – in all the wrong places and all the right places too. Everywhere. The dating scene is rapid. A constant interview.
"Where you from?
"A Scorpio?"
"Fuck it, let's go to bed."
They meet, fall in love, divorce and send hateful text messages before the appetizer arrives.
"It's not me, it's you."
"Have a nice life."
"I'm outta here!"

The places around New York are rushing too. New Jersey, Connecticut... Long Island. Dashing around like nut jobs! Mostly in cars. After they've zoomed around on foot, they get into motored vehicles and rush like ambulance drivers on meth.
"We gotta get there!"
"We're Late"
"We're going to miss the trailers and they're my favorite part!"
Where are they going? Who knows? But they're getting there fast! They have cars that can go 150 miles per second and will do that if necessary.
"I'll see you on the beach in 10 minutes."
But they're 30 minutes away! How will they get there? They don't know. But they can do it. They'll make it

happen. Find the time. If they're not on the beach drinking beers in under 10 minutes, they've failed. They stomp the gas and drive like greased lightning. The speed limit is 40 so they do 90. They must. They've got things to do! They're on a mission! Their word is their bond. They said 10 minutes and by God, they mean 10 minutes. They'll endanger the world. Their car engines are ENORMOUS. It can drive to the moon in 15 minutes. What about the beach? 15 seconds?

They stick their head out the window:

"Get the hell out of my way – I'm going to the beach!"

The tires are barely touching the road. They're fuckin' flying.

"I'm driving over here!"

"Get out, of, the, mother-fucking way!"

"Move!"

How dare the people in front of them drive the speed limit. What are they, stupid? Who drives the speed limit? It antiquated - ancient. No one has driven 30 mph in 50 years! Get the hell out of the way! They're late! On a mission!

They hit the beach and all is right with the world. The core temperature of their engine is 5,000 degrees Kelvin, but that's OK.

"Isn't this the best? Hand me another beer."

"I'm one with the universe."

"Toss the Frisbee?"

New Yorkers even sleep fast. Fast asleep. They crash hard. Hit the sheets. Get some shut eye. They squeeze their eyes shut and try to sleep. Snooze away.

"I'm sleeping here!"

"I've been in bed for three minutes and I can't sleep!"

"I have a big day tomorrow."

"Lots to do!"

Two Ambien and six shots of NyQuil will do the trick. They guzzle it down... out they go. Out like a light. They dream of fast trains, express subways and buffalos running off a cliff. Unstoppable forces.

They awaken fresh as daisies and ready to go. Take on the world! They hit the ground running. Instant breakfast.

"Can't eat."

"Just coffee."

"Gotta MOVE!"

They chug gallons of steaming hot coffee. Rocket fuel. Pure caffeine adrenaline. They kiss everyone goodbye and sprint out the door. Like a 100-yard dash. In the car in seconds. Pedal to the metal. They're catching trains... subways too. The ones in their dreams.

They check their watch 150 times because they're running late! Very late!! The sun hasn't come up yet, but they're late. Half the planet is asleep. Their neighbors too. But they're late! They have meetings and appointments. They're rushing around. Going places.

Where are they going? Nobody knows. Can anyone stop them long enough to ask?

THE SOCIAL NECKWORK

My Grandfather was the world's biggest nerd. I mean that with all due respect. He was pretty much a genius. After World War II, he immediately got a job at Pfizer – the company that gave us the immunity to ward off Covid-19, but also has the ability to wipe out the human race ten thousand times over. While employed there, he helped create a machine that rapidly produced penicillin. It was one of the cornerstones of the company. He worked for Pfizer his whole life and even had his hand in the development in Viagra, which we all know is the greatest achievement in men's erections since porn. When he wasn't at Pfizer, he was in his study doing math and breaking down complex numerical equations that most of us look upon as some kind of alien dialect. These books he read, with pages upon pages of math problems, resembled the raining green code in the film *The Matrix*, except instead of electrifying neon green on black, the stilted black numbers were strewn across boring white paper.

My Grandpa had six children who were, for some cruel twist of fate, all artists. I believe this may have driven him nuts, but he was a fairly quiet man, so no one knows for sure. He spent a lot of time in the garden. I assume he went there to escape the madness of his children. When one can't associate well with humans or animals, plants are the next best option until you go all the way crazy and speak to walls, or at worst, yourself.

They say there's a strong correlation between math and art. The brain works in similar ways when the two things are done. I failed math in 9th grade and was forced to do summer school, so I'm not sure what genius came up with that hypothesis. But, I do believe it on some level. On my father's side of the family, many of the men were either drunken intellectual scientist types or drug-vacuuming artist types. In some cases they were drug-vacuuming intellectual scientists or Drunken Artists. Either way I believe there is something to this math/art phenomenon.

One thing that I have never been mistaken for is an intellectual scientist type. The reason being is instead of having my nose buried in science books, it was buried in drawing pads. One of the great many faults of the men of my family is they are a frustrating lot of know-it-alls. My father, his brothers, his cousins. They seem to know a lot, and because of this, they seem to be an expert on everything. I on the other hand, have realized that there is a wonderful, almost magical sense of freedom to the statement "I don't know." My son asks me a question and I say "I don't know" and we move on with our lives. I realize we can all start talking about land wars, stomach enzymes and the reproductive systems of wolves because we saw an article on the Internet, but perhaps we shouldn't. Nor should we start talking in great detail about these things because we skimmed the headline in a journal or overheard someone mention it at a party. So it's best to say *I don't know* and go back to doing what you were doing... drinking heavily or burning something on the grill.

No matter how much art I do, I still have scientist in the blood. By nature... or by nurture. However you look at it. That's a science debate. I have recently delved into the realm of scientific research totally by accident. My grandfather would have been proud. I haven't broken any complex codes or solved any one of the many unsolvable math problems that have perplexed the eggheads of the world. My research was about a social construct based on allergies.

Growing up, I had terrible allergies. I'm allergic to cats, dogs, pollen, ragweed, bees and many other things. The earth, in its infinite ways, has tried to cripple me with its natural dustings... constricting my lungs, loading me with mucous and choking me with phlegm. As a kid my sinuses were both swollen and hollow, my throat raw and wet, and my eyes glassy and dry. But, worst of all, I would get these absurd, almost laughably long sneezing attacks. Funny when you sneeze 10-11 times, but reach the point of ridiculousness when you hit the high 20s. People laugh at first, then become concerned, then clear the room. It's too much to take. How many sneezes can one person sneeze? My abdomen would quake and I'd fall to the floor like I'd run a marathon. But it's not just the sneezing. Every orifice in my head would drain like a broken fire hydrant. It's not easy to handle for an outside observer. There's tissues and honking and nose-clearing blows. It's a solid ten minutes of nuclear meltdown and when the calm comes, everyone has exited my life.

Because of this terrible affliction, I got weekly allergy shots, two times a week. I'd go to the doctor's office, which was actually an old house... possibly haunted, and I'd get loaded up with all kinds of elixirs. The kindly nurses would shake the vials and tell me what they were loading me up with. They'd stick my skinny arms with syringe-filled allergens and my shoulders would swell with reactive intensity. It was really pretty terrible. But the truth is – it saved me a lifetime of problems. Instead of daily barrages of never-ending sneezing attacks, I'm down to about one every two weeks.

But I still suffer from many other issues. One of those issues is that I'm constantly clearing my throat. It's gotten so bad that I do it all the time whether I need to or not. Like a spasm. I'll say two words, clear my throat, then continue the sentence... which is usually just two or three more words. I close any statement, phrase or idea with a throat-clearing. Sometimes I'll start any statement, phrase or idea with a throat-clearing. Meaning, if I want to ask someone to go for Chinese food, it will have three or four throat-clearings during the process even though the question has no more than five words.

And this is how my social experiment began.

Because there is tremendous power in the throat-clearing, a simple throat-clear can stop an entire room of people murmuring around cocktails to give you their full, undivided attention. Hopefully if you've drawn the eyes of everyone in the room, you have something to say. Usually I don't because I'm never in the position to address a room full of people. But, if I did, it would be to complain about something trivial… like itchy tags on t-shirts or the failure of the world's leaders.

The social experiment began in earnest when I entered a delicatessen and was met by a wall of people. It was a warm summer day and the air was thick. Entering the deli, I was hit with cool air-conditioning and my throat reacted by flooding my esophagus with phlegm, which I cleared with a rattling "A-Hem!" Well, the wall of people turned and apologized to me like I was royalty – parting for me like Moses parted the Red Sea. One woman even stepped aside and held out her arm… inviting me with safe passage through the group and even bowed and motioned as if to say: *If you would you be so kind as to forgive me for blocking your way.* Startled, I held up my hands as to say "Oh, No. I didn't mean it THAT way," but before I could open my mouth, I found myself prancing through the crowd like I was on the Versace catwalk. All because I held my fist to my face and cleared my throat. I realized immediately this neck-hack had a power that should be wielded very carefully.

One day I left my house and there was a guy letting his little toy dog shit on the neighbors' lawn. I caught a face-full of early morning sunshine that threw me off-guard and forced me into a thunderous throat-clearing hack. I shit you not, if I had cocked and fired a shotgun, this guy couldn't have been any more spooked. He collected the poop and scampered away like he was fleeing a coup d'état. His dog's legs were moving so fast they looked like those stagecoach wheels that appear to be going backwards in a blur. The poor man was Indian too. I'm sure I came across as some privileged white guy who doesn't want ANYONE's dog pooping near my house, especially some brown guy and his tiny brown mutt. Again, I held up my hands and made a "No! That's not what I meant" face, but he was halfway down the block at that point. I could have chased him to explain the misunderstanding, but then he'd think I was trying to kill him with a machete or something and that would be worse than the throat-clearing.

Now he probably has my street sectioned off as a no walk zone – a place to never stroll with his dog or his family. It's unfortunate because in another life we could be friends. If he knew the real me, he'd know that I'm a man that accepts all kinds of people... brown, black... phlegmy and non-phlegmy. He and I could watch foreign films together, drink Kingfisher beer and grill Indian things on my bar-b-que. He doesn't realize that I'm married to a Brazilian and have the dating history of the United Nations "About Us" web page. But, it's way too late... the guy is gone and if I check Zillow, his house will be on the market before I take my next scheduled Zyrtec.

The throat-clear is an example of "Pardon Me" that has passed down through time. Depending on the tone, level of sarcasm, anger, or impatience you instill into the throat-clearing, it can get people to do many things. It can get them moving out of the way, begging your forgiveness and on certain occasions, challenging you to a duel. Of course in my naïve head, I thought the throat-clear as social interruption had died with Carey Grant, or any number of Baby Boomer movie idols that I only remember in black and white. But my allergies have shown me that this is absolutely untrue. The throat hack as a communal freeze is alive and well. Jimmy Stewart could stop a dance hall full of people dead in their tracks with a minor hiccup, but I don't wield that kind of power. The frog in my throat has the power of a dog bark, but the bark is much worse than the croak.

Take for example, my use of throat-clearing at the grocery store.

I got on line with five items. The woman in front of me had six. I had to clear my throat, but this time I was totally conscious of the moment. I cleared "A-Hem!" and she turned with a look of embarrassment. She immediately sized up the number of items in *my* arms and the number in *hers*, and insisted I go ahead. To her, my obvious importance trumped her time-crushing pile of items that would slow me to a standstill. I was suddenly a *much* higher priority because I throat-cleared, and she was ready to use herself as a doormat so I could get out of there.

I tried this experiment at the grocery checkout a few weeks later and the woman ahead of me turned and scanned me up and down as though I'd called her a bitch. If I had slapped her with a white glove, she couldn't have been more insulted. With her eyes bugged out at me, her jaw dropped... yet, she kept her mouth closed, forming a face that I can only describe as a magician ready to plop an egg from their mouth. Her expression said, "My god! Who in the hell do you think you are?"

Eventually she turned back to her items and checked out. But there was a real sense of danger... that, perhaps, the next time I throat-cleared against the back of her head, I'd be hearing from her lawyer.

Other times the experiment goes awry. I'll be someplace and clear my throat and people will turn, so I need to show them I'm not inconvenienced with their presence by feigning a coughing attack. I'll hack and cover my mouth until they look relieved. Their eyes soften and I can see them say to themselves: "Oh, he's just coughing. I'm not in his way... THANK GOD!"

Unfortunately when I pretend to have a coughing attack, it dredges up real phlegm in my throat, which causes me to have a *real* throat-clearing attack. If I have a list of chores to do, I'll be hacking at people in checkout lines all day and it's a game of hacking and looking at the ceiling and pretending I'm not inconvenienced by them. It's an exhausting dance. By the time I get home, I have Whooping Cough. This will parlay into endless throat-clearings that could rival an 80 year-old man after a heavy diet of meat and cream. It's like when I take a drink of water and it goes down the wrong pipe and I spend the next three days clearing my throat.

Once an experiment ends, you'd think I learned something, but I learn nothing. In fact, the only thing this experiment leads to was instilling a habit of clearing my throat every time I entered an establishment. Like a Pavlovian trigger mechanism. I hack and people scoot their carts to the side, shuffle quickly and even scram. To compensate, I now clear my throat as quietly as I can. Unfortunately it's a long, arduous task. A firm "A-Hem" will clear the passages quickly. Do it slowly and it's like sucking a milkshake through a straw. To watch me do this, you'd think I was swallowing a fist of peanut butter. My throat bulges as I strain every neck muscle to clear it out. Instead of a fast hack, it now sounds like a man pulling his last, dying breath – a soldier on the battlefield, his buddy hanging over him, their hands clasped.

"Tell my mother I love her.... Arrrgghhhhahhhh."

Before, when I heaved the confident, abrupt "A-Hem," people took notice. With the slow, dying man's gurgle, people take notice, it's just before they turned with anxiety and now they turn with a look of horror.

The slow throat-clearing pull usually leaves me with a mouth full of mucous and nowhere to expel it. I know, this is pretty gross. If you're anything like my wife, you find talk of mucous deplorable. She hates it. When my son was about six months-old, he was so congested in the nose, he was wailing from misery. Rita couldn't relieve him using a nasal bulb, so I snatched him from her arms, cupped my mouth over his nose and sucked his sinuses clean of snot. Instant relief! Rita used every part of her body to control her gag reflexes so she wouldn't toss her cookies. She refused to kiss me for a month after that. 13 years later, I don't think she's fully recovered. When I mention it, she gags and has to turn away. She can't look me in the face.

My son is now growing up and he wants to be a scientist. I suppose these things jump a generation. The Artist/Scientist Leap Frog game. He's interested in helping the earth because he realizes that we're destroying it. He wants to find a way to prevent global warming, create better energy sources and stop pollution. I wonder if he has any interest in throat-clearing allergies and their consequences.

Free from the confines of the stale laboratory environment, the Social Neckwork experiment will continue on in the wild known as the *real* world -- in line at the ATM machine, at hot dog stands and in bars, libraries and theaters. It will be conducted on the rich and the poor... the young and the old. Everyone, really.

I'm not sure if data will ever be compiled and documented and placed into journals or medical papers. It's a living art piece... a jam session that never ends. The members of the band look at one another to see who'll stop playing first, but they continue on and on. My civil probe will have no placebos; only real mucous and conducted with live specimens. No animals will be harmed in the study, but I'm sure a few egos will be challenged. No math will be used either. No beakers or Bunsen burners. No assistants will be necessary. No lab coats or any special access into buildings with armed guards wearing sunglasses. Only what the world gives me... the unsuspecting guinea pigs of the world. You could be one of them.

My grandfather, god rest his soul, would be proud.

It's a Very, Very, Very, Fine House

There're building houses anywhere they can find an empty plot of land. Big houses, little house... all kinds of houses. You could wake one morning to find a three-story monstrosity in your back yard. The new neighbors are looking down at you from the balcony of their complicated deck that's eclipsing the sun. Your tomato garden is wilting and so is your property value.

Turn on the TV and half the shows are about houses. They're building tiny houses on wheels, houses in trees, and houses off the grid. They're built from mud, school buses and anything lying around. These convoluted places have swings that will take you from the bathroom to a crow's nest lookout tower. You can take a shit and flip a pancake simultaneously, while yanking a book off your library shelf. All in front of your guests who are crammed on a bench watching your 55-inch TV that flips into a dining table. The electricity is wind powered, the heat comes from the sun, and the water source is tears of regret.

On HGTV, they're making old houses look new and new houses look old. They're tearing things down and building them back up again. They're adding additions and creating square footage. They'll take a 200 year-old house, coat the walls with beaming white paint, then hang a rusty bicycle up and call it home. The floors look like wood but they're a poly-carbonate plastic made to look like wood. They'll last a thousand years – or at least a few months until the new owners come and tear it all out.

The clients demand white granite kitchen counters and a master bath the size of an ocean liner. They want open spaces and a huge yard for their 15 dogs. They'll insist it be in their current neighborhood and won't pay a dollar over dirt-cheap. Somehow they can afford it even though he's a mime and she's a worm wrangler. Their budget is 1.2 million.

People are flipping houses like water bottles. They take a piece of shit, tear it down, build it like new... using the cheapest materials possible of course, and get a fabulous price for it. It's still a piece of shit, but now it's someone else's problem. The new owner will open the fridge and it will start a chain reaction of events that culminates with a crew of asbestos guys vacuuming their attic to the tune of 35 grand.

Everyone's a house flipping visionary. Most people can't color inside the lines of a child's coloring book, but somehow there's a new wave of Frank Lloyd Wrights. They're knocking down walls and putting 18th century chandeliers in the purple half bath off the kitchen.

The furnishings seem to be a blast to shop for. Antique shops are all the rage. Children's sleds from 1950 will become a dried flower basin, dented knight armor will retire as an umbrella holder, broken wood benches yanked from a house fire can be a fireplace mantle, and a hospital bed rescued from an insane asylum can be a shelving unit. The lumberyard is selling reclaimed wood from a barn older than America. The wood is so old it's petrified, but it looks fantastic nailed to the entryway feature wall. They've installed a gas lamp even though Ben Franklin discovered electricity about 500 years ago.

Tiles are a great way to add character. Kitchen backsplashes are glass and hexagons and rich colors guaranteed to be outdated before the mortar sets. Bathrooms are black and white and occasionally mint green. They're as sterile as a hospital morgue. To add more character, they'll reconstitute a wooden roll top desk into a sink basin – an object that's impossible to clean and will spawn black mold after 5 showers.

Sometimes the house is a contest -- who can impress one owner while angering the spouse. Unfortunately there's always a problem. Yes, they can stuff a support beam in the ceiling for 20 grand, but now the husband can't have the upstairs bathroom spa with the vibrating ass washer. They'll stay because it's a great school district and they can keep their obnoxious mother-in-law in the basement where she belongs.

Man-caves and she-sheds are a must. After house shopping for 15 months, the couple needs personal space or face the inevitable divorce. He needs a beer tap and an air-hockey table and she wants a place to read and a comfy chair to contemplate her loneliness.

The hosts doing these renovation shows talk to the camera a lot. They provide sledgehammers to the homeowners who've not done one iota of physical labor in their lives, asking them to smash into walls where water pipes and electrical wiring are laid side-by-side. Once the walls are open the real problems start. Knob and tube wiring, lead pipes and the corpse of a confederate soldier.

If an engineer comes, it's real trouble. They point and support beams and columns need to be wedged in, as well as other safety structures used to prevent houses from collapsing on people. The homeowners' dream of an unobstructed view from the kitchen, through the dining room, and into the bedroom is ruined by one metal stick in the middle of the TV room. It can be disguised as an ancient Roman column, or boxed in with wood and paired with a side table full of wicker baskets on dusty books.

She wants a total gut job and he wants to do no work at all. He's 6' 9" but can't find a showerhead to stand under. She has dreams of putting her mark on the place, fueled by the 500 magazine clippings she's been mounting into scrapbooks since the day their wedding ended.

For some reason, the house show producers thought the viewing public would enjoy listening to homebuyers drone-on about their house fantasies while strolling through them. They verbally shred every design choice, shriek about closet space for their endless shoes, and won't budge on a must-have feature like mudroom hooks to hang their beekeeping equipment. The mansion is 99.9 percent perfect, but there's no place to park their riding vacuum cleaner so it's a deal breaker.

On the balconies, they eulogize about drinking coffee. Once they move in, they'll drink coffee at the kitchen table like everyone else on the planet. No one has yet to brew a cup of coffee, hike three flights of stairs and climb out a window to drink coffee on a balcony. At 7:00 am, there's half an inch of dew on the chairs and it's 45 degrees outside.

Speaking of outsides, they need attention too. Fire pits with cozy brick chairs, strings of antique lights and a waterfall that filters to nowhere. Toss pillows around it for maximum comfort – hopefully it doesn't rain. It's a great place for a glass of wine and a conversation about your third mortgage. Having a second kitchen on the back porch is wonderful... grill, fridge, stove and sink. Perfect for an outdoor Thanksgiving in the snow. Ice skating can take place on the frozen pool and everyone can warm their feet in the oven.

Mature trees are paired with new shrubs. Slabs of slate are twisted into complicated walkways and quaint lampposts are set at the foot of the driveway. Once they rust they can be brought inside and hung on the wall. One minute the yard is mud, the next it's checkered with green grass boxes. Pergolas are raised, pebble stones are bedded, and little Japanese maples pepper the place. Dig a Koi pond and the samurai will come.

There's international buyers too. A computer developer and his family from Denmark are coming to Arizona and are shocked by the wasted space, while the bank manager from North Carolina and her family are in Sweden lamenting about the size of the European fridge. Where are they going to put their 80-pound roasted pig? The husband will crash into every doorway and the mother will have a breakdown because the dishwasher is a hamster on a wheel.

Of course, you can do it yourself. The DIY. Save a

few bucks. These people supposedly have jobs, but they're banging nails for 14 hours a day. The wife is shining a spotlight on the roof while the husband wrangles aluminum flashing around a chimney at midnight. One wrong step and he'll be a cripple for life – but they're saving thousands!

My neighbor has been working on his own house for years now. The working schedule of his crew seems to fluctuate with the tide. They work outside in the rain and inside when it's sunny. They disappeared for six months the millisecond they wrapped the exterior with that eye-sore Tyvek house wrapping. Then the snow and rain beat it to a pulp. When the flowers popped up, they returned to slab fake shingles over the wrapping while it was still sopping wet.

Rental properties are always good. Serial killers need housing too. The space above the garage was a hobby room, but now it's a rental for college students. They'll eat off the ironing board and sleep in a nook by the window. All three of them. The shower has a dryer and the oven is also a washing machine. It's modern space ingenuity.

Sometimes they break down the cost-saving as they're building the rental. Jam another bed under the water heater and it puts another $1,500 in the pocket. Renters appreciate things like good lighting and breathable air.

Renovations never go as planned. Compromises need to be made. The sink faucet was expensive so they installed the mini showerhead used to wash toy dogs. People have been ripping brass fixtures out of their homes for the past 50 years, but now they're cheap so they're back in fashion. Paired with the roll top desk sink basin, the bathroom looks like a three-masted schooner. It's charming. The husband can wear a skipper's cap while using his vibrating ass washer.

Nut Job

I was standing on a street corner in San Francisco and I looked down and there was a spray-painted message stenciled on the concrete sidewalk stating: *Prostitutes Please Stand Here* and I thought: "Yeah, I think I can vibe with San Francisco." Not because I was into soliciting prostitutes, although I do think prostitution should be legal. It was more about someone designating an area for prostitutes and clients to meet and that's modern ingenuity for you in a nutshell. A whore locator system. Useful for everyone. Sort of like an app, but way before smart phones were invented. That's a city full of progressive thinkers... my kind of people.

Coincidentally, that street corner was a trebuchet shot away from Silicon Valley, where the cell phone would essentially rise from the sand and become the ultimate hub of communication where all kinds of apps would connect all kinds of people – prostitutes, Johns and other professionals who wanted to perform fun and interesting acts on each other – both legal and potentially criminal.

After I read the sidewalk message, I crossed the street, but had the sneaking suspicion I was going in the wrong direction, so I popped my head into a corner bar to ask. It was 11:00 am and the place was filled with transsexuals – all of them made up and gorgeous. They were propped like starlets on the bar, twisting their hips on swivel stools, and dressed in short shorts and skin-tight halter tops. It was steaming Africa hot that day, so it made sense. I asked them if, "the San Francisco Institute of Art is this way?" pointing down the hill… maybe south, and they all pointed in the opposite direction – uphill… probably north.

Then, a pretty Asian tranny who was bouncing on her hip at the jukebox, pursed her lips and flapped her eyelashes and said, "Come have a drink with us." I said "I can't I have to meet my friend for lunch" and they all said, "aaawww" in disappointment, which was very flattering, but also tuneful, as it was in unison. But it was true; I had to keep moving. I was running late. And even though I was a degenerate, I very rarely drank before noon, regardless of anyone's sexual orientation or identity.

It was my first time in 'Frisco, visiting my buddy Kevin and his girlfriend Rachel. Kevin was at his office and Rachel was working at the university and she would be free for lunch, so I was hot-footing it to meet her. I climbed up the hill, which was so steep I almost needed a pickaxe and rope – like some kind of Swedish mountaineer – until I reached the top. I'm surprised most San Franciscans don't have massive, bulging calves. The hills are that steep.

Eventually I found myself going downhill, quickly, arriving at the SFU of Art. I bopped around and eventually found Rachel. She was manning the university bookstore checkout counter and scrambling around like a mad woman. We were going to eat in a sunny outdoor spot, but she told me:

"I have to work a double shift because the girl who's supposed to take the next shift is sick. But more like hungover."

And I said, "aaawwww" in disappointment, just like the transsexual girls at the bar.

Rachel possessed many gifts, one being she knew a bullshit story when she heard one, and she wasn't pleased to be left alone at the shop. I told Rachel I could bring her something to eat, when we were interrupted by a teacher who burst into the shop like a man swatting away a cluster of bees.

"Rachel!" He huffed with a frenzied case of the vapors. "My life model didn't show for class and we need a back-up, quick!"

Rachel was not prepared for this news and looked at him stone-faced.

"By the time we call and get someone, your class will be over."

He faced the wall and crossed his arms, as if the answer would be there in the dense cinderblocks.

"I'll do it" I heard myself saying.

"You will?!" he beamed, spinning to face me as the storm cloud of bees lifted.

"Sure."

"It pays a hundred and twenty five dollars." He assured me. "I'm Jonah."

"No problem, Jonah. I'm A.J." and we shook hands.

"Rachel," He squealed, "give A.J. model release papers."

"Sure."

"A.J., meet me in room 115!" I heard him sing as his voice trailed off down the hall.

Rachel smirked. "Oh, he's going to *love* this class today."

I entered room 115 to a horseshoe of students blinking and smiling at me like I was on the receiving end of a rumor. There was a chair in the center of them – alone and unoccupied. Jonah clasped his hands and invited me in.

"Here's our model; this is A.J.!" Everyone clapped. I believe that was my first ovation.

Where should I undress?" I asked, looking for a curtained corner or an adjacent door.

"Right here." He said pointing to the middle of the room.

"Here?" I asked confused.

"It's no problem." Jonah said nonchalantly.

Sure, no problem for *him*... he wasn't getting naked.

There was no robe or curtain or any privacy whatsoever.

I realized quickly the operation might not have been totally legit. That maybe, just maybe, Jonah saw me roaming the halls and wanted to get me undressed. Smart move if that was the case. I believe that theory was solidified when Jonah raced around the room and tossed charcoal and drawing boards into people's laps like they were molten iron from a forge. I'm not even sure this was an art class at all. The blond girl directly in front of me was wearing white designer clothes and not prepared to handle blackened, cloth-killing drawing material in any way. A quick scan of the room revealed the same for all the students.

I shrugged, dropped my clothes and within seconds, I was sitting naked in the chair. Jonah placed a spotlight on me and before long, the students were scratching away, keenly aware of my lights, shadows, and the negative space around me, and not my penis *at all*.

Jonah pranced around observing me like an 8 year-old would do if you told them to act like an art professor -- hand on his chin and occasionally making some profound point about proportions and shading. After he crossed my view a few times, it was clear Jonah was a student teacher... perhaps even younger than me.

At one point Jonah grabbed the spot light and moved it towards my side and closer, which is something you shouldn't do to a group of artists who are in the middle of shading the shadows of a life drawing. He marked, "Look how deep the shadow goes here" and touched my armpit hair.

He snapped his hand back and quickly realized he shouldn't go there. But, he got his one jolly touch out of the experience, and I was officially a nude life model.

•••

About a month after I got home to Long Island, I'd completely forgotten about the modeling job until a check came in the mail for 125 smackers. It was easy money because all I had to do was sit in a chair – something I'd been doing my whole life. Of course I had no clothes on, but that's why the money is so good. Most people are uncomfortable sitting completely naked around a group of strangers while the strangers are completely clothed. For reasons I can't explain, I have no problem with it. I don't get off on being naked with clothed people. I don't thrive on it. But, I'm not ashamed. If my dick is hanging out in the breeze and people see it… it's ok by me. I don't send unwanted dick pics or whip open a trench coat and flash people in the street. But my public nudity is fine – especially when it pays.

Strangely enough, I still get those weird dreams where I'm naked in a room full of people and I'm mortified from embarrassment. I suppose if someone in the dream handed me a check for my nudity, I'd nod and be OK with it. But usually these nudity dreams are anxiety dreams and payment rarely occurs.

The last time I gave unwanted penile attention was when I was 6 and my sister was sitting on our front stoop with her friends when I came to the glass storm door, dropped my shorts and mashed my tiny pee-pee against the glass. Caroline went "eeewwww!" and within seconds, my mother snatched me away, smacked my ass and tossed me in my room.

Sometimes I whip out my bits and show my wife, but she's seen them before and it doesn't conjure up the same thrill it once did. My discipline with my penis is strong. It comes out only when it's asked to do so, either by me or someone else.

Truthfully, I don't have a massive dong to show off to

the world. I think if anything, it's a totally average size. I have been told my junk is good-looking, by the fact that the ratio of length to width are proportionate, so I have that going for me.

Once in a while I'd go to the nude beach with some girl friends. The freedom is quite nice. Most of the people at the nude beach are people you'd never want to see naked even if they were the last human beings on earth -- even for reproductive purposes, so an unwanted erection is never an issue.

Because the thrill of receiving 125 bucks had flooded my veins, I went on a mission to secure more money with my nakedness. I didn't have far to go. I went a few blocks to Joe Mack's art studio in town. It was the private art school I attended as a kid where I drew nude models myself. The studio was an ancient barn on Huntington Harbor, surrounded by boats, dingys, buoys and enough ancient dock wood to give every home decorator on HGTV a raging orgasm. I believe the studio was originally anything from a fishing boat storage house, to an old fish hanging station. Whatever it was, it was one careless cigarette ash from bursting into flames, causing a chain reaction that would rankle the nerves of every insurance agent from Maine to Florida.

I went to the studio to meet Joe after I called on the phone to tell him my deal. We talked about me being a former student, and that I was interested in nude modeling. Although I didn't have the rippling masses of flesh that inspired Michelangelo to pick up a hammer and whack shards of marble off a block into glorious human figures, I had enough meat on my bones to inspire a piece of broken charcoal or two. Serendipitously, Joe was desperate for fresh bodies as one of his more dependable models was pregnant and couldn't stand up anymore. So I was good enough!

The summer started and I was one of three models. There was Michelle, a rumpled bag of flesh who was about 60, with a nice, lean face, framed by a mane of grey hair whose body eventually pyramided into a sack until her cankles melted over her feet. Rounding out the trio was Argo, a circle of a man about 70 years-old. Argo had an athletic Santa face and beard, but was more likely to play the roll of snowman than have children sit on his lap. He used a long stick as a posing prop... depicting himself as the last bastion of protection against an oncoming squad of intruders, and sometimes, a pensive wizard protecting the mouth of a mountain passage.

In San Francisco, I sat in a chair for two hours and it was easy money. This time I stood. But not for an hour or two. I stood, in one position... without moving, for three hours, every Wednesday night, for three months. That was it. I wasn't whipping around like Adonis, flexing my rippling back muscles. I wasn't doing any quick 10-second, *Mr. Universe* poses as the students warmed up with brisk pencil flicks. I stood in one spot for three months and it was the most tedious task I'd ever done in my life.

I didn't move, but the students did. They came in shifts. The first month, the charcoal drawing students drew me; the next month the sculpture people came and sculpted me; and then finally the painters came and painted me. All while I stood in the exact same position.

One evening while I was in town getting soup – which most people don't eat during the hot summer because it's summer, a group of five girls in the sculpture group came into the soup place. The place also sold pretzels, so they were there for pretzels. I recognized one girl because she had big beautiful eyes and stood right in my line of vision in class. She was also the most vocal person in class. She complained that I was too skinny and didn't have enough body mass to sculpt with. She also sculpted my spiky hair like a head full of Medusa snakes, so the realism of her sculpture transformed into a twisty, interpretive piece as the month progressed.

The conversation she and I had went like this:

"Oh hi!" she said enthusiastically.

"Oh, hello." I said as I waved goodbye with my soup.

But the conversation in my head went more like this:

"Oh hey... you're the model guy whose penis we see in class every Wednesday."

"Yes, I'm the guy whose penis you see all the time."

"Okay, well... see you and your penis on Wednesday."

"Yes, take care. I'll show you my penis on Wednesday."

And then I left. The girls smiled like Cheshire Cats as I exited. They were being flirty, but they were all 17 and I was 26, which made it a bit creepy on my part... but I looked 18, so maybe it all balanced out.

As the summer was coming to a close, the August heat and humidity cranked up. The windowless barn didn't have air conditioning, and the humming, metallic floor fans just circulated everyone's warm body air around the interior. The painting teacher, Judith was walking around and commenting on her student's work – dispensing little nuggets of hushed critique as she hopped from one canvas to the next. As Judith stood right in my line of sight, she adjusted her glasses and pointed at the student's canvas and said:

"Look at his knee and look at the shadow...."

And then there was a *really* long pause.

Like, uncomfortably long.

I began to panic. When I modeled, I'd play albums in my head to keep my brain occupied. I'd envision a record on a turntable and play a famous album, song for song, from memory, like I was listening to it with headphones. But Judith's pause was enough to scratch the needle off the record. My brain returned to the room and I looked at Judith whose mouth was agape. The student, who of course was a female, had also stopped to take a long and awkward glance.

"Jesus," I thought. "Did I go too far into my head?" Up until then I'd been professional and refrained from any, boners, hard-ons, Braunschweigers, tent poles, chubbies, schwings, shifts, shafts, windmills, moray eels, bulges, tube steaks, loose canoes, 9-irons, pool noodles, snake charmers, submarines, heat seeking missiles, fatties, lead pipes, stiffies, twirling batons, pork loins, upper-cuts, engorgements, Luciano Pavarottis or even a full-on Moby Dick.

But Judith's hesitation had me in a panic. I didn't want to make a scene, so I bent my neck slightly and glanced down using only my eyes.

Let me give you a brief synopses of the male penile anatomy in case you're unfamiliar. The average body temperature is 98.6 degrees Fahrenheit (37 C), but the male testicles prefer the cooler temperature of 93.2 (34C). When the man's body is too warm, the testicles and scrotum drop, and when the testicles are too cool, the scrotum will tighten and rise towards the body to warm themselves. It's quite a fascinating little elevator system.

So, in this sweltering summer heat, I look down and my freakin' nuts are about midthigh. They look as if someone knocked two billiard balls to the bottom of a knee sock and hung it between my legs. But only after the sock had been swung over their head a few times to really stretch the thing out. The *boys* were just above my knee... a distance I didn't think they could achieve in their lifetime, and certainly never would unless I was standing around naked for hours in the summer heat.

Judith *finally* continued her sentence... and I flipped *Sgt. Peppers* to side two and sang along. There was nothing else to do. I calmly retreated to my inner world and hoped everyone had taken sex education classes.

The summer sessions ended without incident and I continued posing into the Fall on Saturday mornings for student portfolio classes. Saturday morning was the easiest class to pose for because I was usually drunk from the night before. I never had an issue with nude modeling, but if I ever did feel modest or slightly shy, it was washed into oblivion by a drunken hangover.

The additional cash was such a help, I moved to New York City shortly after. Once in Manhattan, I searched in vain for nude modeling jobs, but there were absolutely none to be had. Apparently, New York City is chock full of people who enjoy getting naked -- some of them for free. So my hopes of extra nude modeling money were blown away into the naked wind.

WHO WANTS TO BE A BARTENDER?

John McEnroe was the bad boy of the tennis world in the early 1980s. He was infamous for shouting at the chair umpires and questioning whether they needed the use of eyeglasses, their judgments being so careless in their calls against him. He'd cry "You can't be serious!" and slam his racquet down in anger - which would splinter into pieces because rackets were still made of wood. Many considered John a pain in the ass and at times, an insufferable jerk. I'm totally fine with him and honestly, consider him a great human being – mainly because after my son Max was born, he was forced to stay in the hospital for a week with a terrible case of Jaundice. Relieving the stress of this stay was the fact he stayed in the John and Patty McEnroe Neonatal care unit of Lenox Hill Hospital on the upper east side of Manhattan. The total cost of the stay was absolutely free.

Someone whose NICU stay was NOT free was my wife. Rita did not meet the age requirements to stay in the neonatal unit, as one might surmise. Her five-day stay was toughed out in the normal wing of the hospital, where they serve horrible food, ignore you completely, and the breath of death is lurking around every corner. She was gutted deep with a C-section that debilitated her for months. Getting her out of the hospital in five days was a challenge in itself.

When it was time for my son to come home, he was handed over to me – a bundle of joy. I was also handed the hospital bill, which was a bundle of sadness. The bill was a whopping $120,000. When I opened it, I blinked so many times you would have thought I was having a seizure. Maybe I was. I was hoping my eyes were out of whack and needed to be blinked into focus because there were so many zeros at the end. But nope, all the zeros were legitimate. I asked the hospital for an itemized list so I could see the extraneous padding they added to the bill. Things like "Nurse turned on the light - $400" and "Aspirin - $250." When they sent me the itemized bill, it somehow had been reduced a stunning $36,000 to a REASONABLE $84,000. I suppose even THEY couldn't justify some of the absurd charges they'd jammed in there. Then my health insurance, which I believe was being run out of the back of a rusty van in a Costco parking lot, took a stab at the costs. That didn't do too much to chop it down. But those pesky charges you hear so much about like '$250 to turn the lights on and off' were still lingering about.

After a phone call consisting of some firm stances, a small amount of shouting, world-class haggling, and another run through insurance, I got the bill down to what one would consider manageable, but still enough to send most people into a lifetime of debt... $64,000.

My buddy Kevin had a son a few years before Max came into the world. William required open-heart surgery and the bill for that delicate procedure was a heart-stopping $1,000,000. Kevin took that bill and framed it. What else could he do? He didn't have a million lying around, so he stuck it under glass, hung it on the wall and waited for someone to knock on his door and dare to collect the money. So in comparison, my 64K seemed like a drop in the bucket. Still, when someone hands you a million dollar invoice, the normal reaction is to double-over and laugh at the absurdity of it all. But, when the cost is $64,000, there's a sense that it could and probably SHOULD be paid. It's not funny. Just scary.

So I did what anyone in my shoes would do when they're scrambling to pool together 64 grand… I went onto everyone's favorite primetime game show in 2010, *Who Wants To Be A Millionaire?*

I've always been a huge trivia buff. *Jeopardy!* has remained a constant not only on my television, but on the game show and television landscape in general. It's a part of our culture as much as anything—perhaps even more than *The Simpsons* or *60 Minutes*. I mean, how many people can hum the *Jeopardy!* theme without batting an eye? *Jeopardy!* is a pretty difficult trivia show, but once in a while they'll feature a category for dumb-asses like me. Categories like "Movies" or "Sports" or something random like, "80s Music." I tend to knock those out of the park. Most of the time though, I'm either scratching my head in perpetual perplexity or trying to convince myself that Alex Trebek (now Ken Jennings) was speaking a different language.

Millionaire is filmed in New York City, so I went onto their website to see if I could try out, get on the show, and earn some hard-earned (fast) cash. Serendipitously, they had an upcoming "Movie Week" edition and were scheduling interviews for contestants. Movies! Something I actually know a lot about! On *Jeopardy!*, the categories are like "15th Century Monarchs" or "Bible Quotes"… things I know absolutely nothing about. But movies? I can movie trivia in my sleep. I could never do *Jeopardy!* anyway, regardless of the category. One of my biggest faults is not being able to finish reading the answer before one of the contestants gives the question. (for those who don't know the show, they give you the answer and you answer with a question, in the form of a question). I have attention issues and sometimes my mind wanders off as the answer/question is being read. I also don't trust listening to the host read off the question because I have listening issues as well—so Ken Jennings talking and me reading simultaneously, tend to conflict. That leads to me blurting out an embarrassingly wrong answer. Like when they ask for the capital of a state and I answer the name of the state instead. That's a common boner on my part. So *Jeopardy!* will never work for me.

I also could never be on *Wheel Of Fortune* either. These two shows have been running back to back in New York for decades and they're as synonymous as gin and tonic. When I was a kid, I was convinced when the crowd collectively yelled "Wheel! Of! Fortune!" at the beginning of the show, they were actually yelling "Wheel! Of! Torture!" (if you listen closely, it's totally what they say.) I've had a love/hate relationship with *Wheel Of Fortune* my whole life.

Mostly because the contestants on the show are so incredibly stupid. Someone always solves the puzzle after earning $650 and there's still four B's left on the board. That shit drives me insane! I wonder if people actually know how to play the game before they come on the show. I assume they do because – why else would they be there?

Millionaire is Jeopardy! for dumbasses. You can rake in mounds of cash for a half hour of work, where Jeopardy! requires you to ride a 3 week nerd gamble to earn a few bucks, and Wheel earns you pocket change in comparison. Both shows film in California and since I was already down $64,000, I wasn't about to hop a flight to Burbank any time soon. So I filled out an online form and submitted my application to Millionaire. A few weeks later, I got an email to "come on down" and try out.

•••

The try-outs were at 6:00pm on the Upper West Side of Manhattan, an easy bus ride across Central Park on the 79th street line that dropped me off somewhere in the 80s. It was the middle of Summer and it was a super hot day as the sun steamed the west side in a late afternoon broil. I stood in line with a bunch of other random people… all of them stupid and not worthy of getting on the show, according to me and my superior brain-power. They'd come in all shapes and sizes. Older black women, young Hispanic kids, and goofy looking white guys. I was in the goofy white guy category if that wasn't abundantly clear.

A show runner strolled the street and took our names

and checked identification. Eventually, we went through a studio side door and into a room. The room wasn't any different than a corporate meeting space you might find at the Gary, Indiana Ramada Inn. All of us, about 50 people in total, sat at a school desk and were given a paper test and pencil. When prompted, we flipped the page and went at it – a multiple-choice exam with 30 questions. They varied from films of the past, Academy Award winners, to documentaries released just a few weeks before the test. I somehow got every question correct and was one of 10 people asked to stay for an "interview."

Even though I love *Jeopardy!*, my absolute least favorite part of each show is the interview portion. I actually find it quite torturous. On *Wheel*, the people are a bit more tolerable because they're happy and decent people with husbands or kids or dogs and jobs. But on *Jeopardy!*, the contestants are either horribly boring or harboring some strange pent-up nerd anger. The reason they're so boring is because most of these people have been staring at books and calculating numbers their entire lives. Many seem incapable of talking to a human unless it's in the form of a question.

"So, it says here Simon that you once played checkers for 12 hours straight? Tell me about that."

"That's right. Back in college, my roommate Eugene and I shared a beer and hunkered down for a tour-de-force checkers session which lasted approximately 12 hours and seven minutes."

"And who, may I ask, won?"

"Let's just call it a tie." (bad forced chuckle)

Obviously before the show starts, the contestants fill

out a list of subjects they'd be willing to chat with the host about. But these folks are as stimulating as the Dewey Decimal System. Instead of getting insight into their lives, it shines a spotlight on their pitifully awkward existence. I don't feel sorry or begrudge these people in any way. They are who they are. The world is made up of all kinds of people. But I don't necessarily want to know more about them. I'd prefer if *Jeopardy!* announcer Johnny Gilbert just announced their names and their occupation at the beginning of the show and leave it at that.

"From Tuscaloosa Alabama, a water conservation engineer, Robert Svengilikis."

That's it. That's all I need to know about the guy. Let's play the game and keep things moving till the *Final Jeopardy!* questions/answers are revealed.

On *Who Wants To Be A Millionaire?* we're forced to watch the contestants "talk out" their answers throughout the entire show. In fact, it's encouraged. But that can be even more excruciating than anything *Wheel* and *Jeopardy!* has to offer. Instead of the show being the star of the show, the *contestant* is the star of the show. Talk about the inmates running the asylum! Sometimes these people have the most bizarre thought processes and tend to be obnoxious. The show wants people who can babble a constant stream of completely unconnected thoughts so host, Meredith Vieira can knock zippy one-liners off of them. It's not entertaining if we're not laughing AT THEM.

After the movie test, everyone who passed was asked to stay and everyone else exited with no parting gifts. I was approached by a small blond woman who was confident and seasoned. I know this because she spoke to me like I might be someone who was either dangerous or brain damaged. She sat me down along a row of tables and chairs against the back of the room with five other potential contestants, all packed together with their interviewers. She began to ask me questions about myself. So did the other four interviewers to their potential contestants and suddenly there was a bombast of blather. All of us trying to show our interviewers that we had a glowing charm that would be *perfect* for television.

unfortunately, something happened to me during the process. I started to wither. Three months of late night baby feedings, 9 to 5 workdays and the unforgiving summer heat finally caught up to me right then and there, and my brain turned to pudding. I simply could not get my energy up and came across like a lobotomy recipient. The guy next to me was being so overly-enthusiastic, he seemed to be trying out for *Who wants to Be a Wrestling Heel?* He shouted his answers and cackled after each one like a man possessed by the ravages of a cocaine binge.

In comparison, I seemed like a wallflower. I spoke softly about being a new father and my exciting life as a graphic designer. That was the death knell. I was more in tune to the nerds of *Jeopardy!* than the yapping, detective-process thinkers of *Millionaire*. A week later, I received an email that I would not be appearing on the special "Movie Week" edition of *Millionaire*. My dreams of paying off my debt and being on a trivia show were dashed in one electronic message.

•••

My next attempt at some fast cash was to do something that unfortunately didn't come in eye-popping monetary increments that doubled until it reached a million dollars — bartending.

I went to Craigslist and searched for some quality bartending jobs, but was met with nothing but bartending schools who'd place you like a robot into a hotel lounge where you'd be expected to make every drink known to mankind. If some chic, high-society barfly comes in and asks me for Puss-cafe or some kind of Gin-fizz, I'd be forced to make it and do it while they stared at me like a kid watching his ice cream cone being piled.

My libation work history was limited to bars where the most complicated drink I made was either a Cosmopolitan or a Margarita. Mostly, I worked in joints where the most laborious thing I did was pop a beer and poured shots with a bottle snatched from the speed rack. So bartending placement jobs weren't going to work for me.

One place finally did pop up through the Craigslist filter. A freshly opened bar in Spanish Harlem on Lexington and 104th street. I sent an email and it was answered almost immediately. I went to the bar for an interview and I believe I was hired before the door closed behind me upon entering. Run by a short and handsome El Salvadorian named Raoul, the bar was opened with the intent to infuse some downtown East Village gentrified charm into a neighborhood of mostly Central Americans. Raoul was tired of the insistent Bachata music that rang through every place in Spanish Harlem and attracted, and I paraphrase: "cheap-skate, one and done drinkers who complained about the strength of their drinks and tried to ride a cocktail all night by hounding the bartender for more alcohol in their drink."

He'd already hired a white manager named Chris, who was determined to make a playlist rotation based on Coldplay and bands of their ilk. Raoul had already stocked the bar with an eclectic group of bartenders before I arrived on the scene. A handsome Hispanic guy named Benny, a tall black model named Jennie and a duo of tattooed Spanish and white girls, Alex and Michelle. All he needed to complete the band was a blond, spiky haired white dude and I seemed to fit the description. So I started immediately the following Thursday night.

I was given some fairly choice spots on the calendar. A Thursday night shift, a Friday Happy Hour which could parlay into the night depending on the momentum of the crowd, and a Sunday afternoon slot.

Immediately, I knew what Raoul was trying to do with his bar and the challenges that lay before him. As the Thursday evening work crowd filtered in, the place was soon packed. Me and Juanita, a down to earth single mother, slung drinks to a rabid crowd. For every drink order I took, I received two orders to change the grunge rock music to Bachata music… something I was told, no matter how many times I was asked, not to do.

As the first hour passed, I received not one, not two, but three drunken pleas, from two women and a man, that I'd simply not given them ANY alcohol in their drinks. "I can't taste anything in here!" they demanded as they shook their heads incredulously. " I don't think you put alcohol in here at all!"

Being my first shift, I topped-off all of their drinks. But when the toothless Hispanic grandmother came back for seconds... convinced that I'd served her water, I was forced to turn her away. That rejection was met with a full-on ban by her. She turned, rotated her hand as if signaling a mob, and had five people march out in protest behind her.

Juanita couldn't stand the demands for Bachata music and turned the dial to Bachata music. Almost immediately, Chris the manager walked in for his 8:00pm watch and was angry to hear the insistent guitar beat of South American music wafting through the place. He immediately cranked the dial to crunchy guitar noise that was met with a Bronx cheer, the likes of which I hadn't heard since the Boston Red Sox were last in town.

Before happy hour ended, I was approached by a well-dressed Hispanic man who put his arm around me and carefully explained the neighborhood demographic and why they demanded Bachata music. He ended his firm stance by telling me I needed to do what was right for the neighborhood and that this "White grunge music wasn't going to fly around here." I told him I understood completely. I also knew that he was confusing me with Chris because he kept calling me Chris. The only resemblance Chris and I had was a scruffy beard, but other than that, we were completely different looking. I told the guy I was not Chris the manager, but A.J. the bartender. The guy shook his head like I was an idiot and said, "Yes, I know, I want you to relay this information to Chris." Chris was literally standing right there in the conversation huddle with us and stated with frustration, "I can't play Bachata music, Raoul doesn't want it played in here." That info was met with a headshake and a dismissive hand-wave by the well-dressed Hispanic man, followed by, "I'll speak to Raoul myself."

Raoul of course, wasn't hearing any of it. He was doggedly determined to turn the place into a sophisticated cocktail lounge. So determined that the following week, he bought the recently shuttered nail salon next door and blew a hole through the wall to connect the places. He filled that space with candlelit tables and offered waiter service. The bar didn't even have a name. The only way you could tell it was a bar was if you stuck your face against the front glass and squinted into the darkened cavern. Unfortunately, the nail salon space was a zoning violation and he needed to close the wall up. The bar was once again a small box that was really too small for much of anything. It had one couch and coffee table and the bar itself could only accommodate about 10 stools. When the place was jammed, it violated every code New York City had to offer.

Juanita was a saving grace to me. Not only was she sweet and gave me a baby gift for my son, she was a buffer to the semi-hostile crowd. I was not always met with affection from the Hispanic clientele. At times, people were openly hostile to me. Much of that was because they thought I was Chris. Again, we bearded white dudes tend to look the same and the fact that Chris was running a swank, Bachata-less hipster drinking hole in the middle of red beans and rice territory was met with uninterrupted insurgence.

My favorite shift was the easy, breezy Sunday shift. The crowd was easy-going and mellow. A Japanese opera singer named Ichiro, who was obsessed with gospel music, would come in and drink till he needed to lean on his friend and translator Duncan. Ichiro sang in black churches around Harlem and found a saving grace in the bar. He grilled me about America and all the wisdom I could offer. Ichiro also loved the Mexican food that would be delivered from across the street from Raoul's friend Hector.

Hector was about five foot eight and 275 pounds — a bull of a man who I'm convinced had never smiled in his life. He'd wander over from the restaurant, come behind the bar, grab a soda and stand behind me like a statue. It was as uncomfortable as it sounds. Hector was not a man to be fucked with. He was a businessman, running a good Mexican restaurant and was putting in a million hours a week. He was tired, raw, and without mirth. I once asked him if he was inspired to open a restaurant because of his family's cooking and he walked away and said "No" with such gloom, you'd have thought I'd asked if he enjoyed human flesh for breakfast.

When Hector wasn't breathing down my neck, Raoul's "liquor delivery man" would come about two or three times a shift. A non-English speaking man of about 60, the delivery man would limp up to the bar smiling, nodding, and winking at me like we were part of a secret alliance of mixologists. He'd make his way behind the bar, look down and magically produce a fresh bottle of vodka and place it at my feet. He'd rub his fingers together – the universal "money" sign, and say "twenty." I told him it wasn't my job to pay for the deliveries and he'd nod, wink and touch his nose and say "Raoul" and leave. Then he'd return a few hours later with a bottle of Tequila, delivered at my feet, with the same wink and nod ritual.

Sundays didn't provide the bread I needed to make the shift worthwhile, but it was serene enough to make the crazed Thursday and Friday night shift more tolerable. One person I rarely saw was Raoul himself. The only time I saw him was at closing time to lock the place up. He'd pull up in his convertible with Jennie, the stunning black model who didn't seem to work there anymore and command us to "hurry up and sweep." Considering Raoul was married with two daughters, riding around with Jennie seemed like a recipe for disaster.

One upcoming Friday night shift, Juanita asked me to switch with her Saturday shift and when I arrived for that, I was told someone was shot and killed in front of the bar the night before – during my regular shift. I looked down to see drops of blood, and what I could only determine to be the scraping of metal rods into the cement sidewalk. As one can imagine, it gave me an uneasy feeling. I was happy to earn a few extra bucks, but I didn't want to die in the process. Yes, a few hundred bucks a week will help the family out, but it's useless to them if I'm dead.

I clung to the job for another month, but as the Autumn air grew considerably cooler, I was preparing myself to quit. Fortunately, I didn't have to quit because Raoul closed the bar to "rework the concept" as he said. Chris had already quit... unable, or perhaps, unwilling to fight the customers about the choice of music. Raoul told me he'd contact me for a job once the bar reopened, but that call never came.

It was for the better. I was burning the candle at both ends. Between 3:00am feedings, a 9 to 5 job and a bartending gig that had me slinging drink to angry customers... some of them armed and dangerous, I was feeling the weight of the world.

Tragically, I was never able to pay that hospital bill and it went to collections. I never received a call from Raoul, but I got daily calls from the collection agency who hounded me to pay the bill until it broke my sanity. I eventually put the charges on credit cards, which strained my finances until I filed for bankruptcy.

The American health care system... gotta love it.

J-E-T-S JETS! JETS! JETS!

I have eclectic taste. I love Fellini movies, wistful jazz music that makes me melancholy, and extremely dense biographies… but only up to the part where the person got famous, then I'm out. I'm also one of those assholes who believes we should have the Monday after the Super Bowl reclassified as a holiday so we can all nurse our debilitating hangovers.

Super Bowl Sunday is like Christmas to me. I turn on the TV at 11 a.m. and listen to the talking heads scream at each other about every story they can bleed from each players' tragic life no matter how insignificant it is. Sometimes I'll leave the room at noon to the sounds of Terry Bradshaw analyzing a quarterback performance, and return at 3:00 to the sounds of Terry Bradshaw ranting about a wide receiver, and it's as if he never took a breath. Terry Bradshaw won four Super Bowls with the Pittsburg Steelers in the 1970s and he's pretty much a hero.

I became a fan of the New York Jets on January 20,

1980. I know this because it was during the Super Bowl. While watching Super Bowl XIV (that's the number 14 for those who don't know Roman Numerals or Super Bowls) I wandered into my grandparents' den to a crowd of people watching the big game. I hadn't yet decided who my team was. I surveyed the room and there was a mix of opinions. The Steelers was the option a drunken reveler named Bobby suggested while strewn across the floor in front of the crackling fireplace. Since they were right there on the TV, ripping the Los Angeles Rams a new asshole, it seemed like an easy choice. But the majority chose The New York Jets, specifically my uncle Chip, who later abandoned the Jets to become a Miami Dolphins fan in one of the most disgusting displays of family betrayal since Michael Corleone took his brother Fredo fishing in *Godfather: Part II*. I chose the Jets as my team and stood firmly behind my choice.

It was the worst decision of my life.

I could have gone for the Steelers right then and there – landing my plane onto the perpetual runway of joy as the Steelers have been in contention for a Super Bowl almost every single one of the 40 years since that day. Instead I landed my plane at LaGuardia Airport, New York – an airport so poor, asylum seekers from war-torn countries book a flight back from whence they came thinking they'd landed in a third world country.

But, we were a family of Jets fans through and through. My destiny was paved in green and white before I knew it. In their finished basement, my grandparents had one of those giant head pictures of Joe Namath you see rendered at street fairs. Except this one was high-class – oil pastel painted on grey Bristol board... Joe's drooping, dreamy eyes following you around the room like the Mona Lisa. My grandmother professed an open crush on Broadway Joe – and who could blame her? The man was the first Rock Star athlete of the times. He won Super Bowl III after guaranteeing it, signed record-breaking money contracts, and did pantyhose commercials on TV. He was tall, dark and handsome – things professed to be of the highest trait in a man at those times. He also had eyes the size of ping-pong balls, the slouch of a man carrying an 80-pound sack of clams on his back, and teeth like extra minty Chiclets. To each his own.

Nevertheless, by 1980, the New York Jets 1969 Super Bowl luster was riding on fumes. My family and their friends were too drunk to notice. They were all riding high on Namath glory and drinking the Kool-Aid. Namath was long gone and his back-up, Richard Todd was manning the quarterback position behind a team that was starting to resurge with one of the all-time great defenses in the history of the game. The New York Sack Exchange. But before that could occur, my father slipped in under the radar and bought four season tickets at dirt-cheap prices in the upper deck of Shea Stadium.

Built in 1960, Shea Stadium sat idly at the edge of Flushing Bay in Queens, a stone's throw away from LaGuardia Airport. The place was rocked by plane reverberations every 5 minutes and by 1970, the state-of-the-art Shea Stadium was a cement toilet bowl, albeit, still beloved by Mets and Jets fans all through the Long Island community. The lower seats would pivot into a V to accommodate the Mets baseball diamond, then in the cold months, would rotate into a rectangle to accommodate a football field. Along with poor drainage, simple framework design, and constructed next to a funnel of cold, hard winds, Shea devolved into a complete dump. Ramps and staircases would collect wrappers, bags, and rain, forming sewage-like garbage piles that never seem to evaporate. The natural grass field became a mud pit, where chunks of green could be seen peeking through the brown as well as the occasional white yardage marker line.

Because of this environment, games felt like a gladiator show for the working class. Football jerseys weren't really an item yet, and most attendees came wearing whatever clothing they wore on a day-to-day basis. When winter weather set in, the stands were a wash of brown coats, muddy green hats, with smatterings of construction worker oranges and yellows. An open-air stadium right on the water made for some brutally harsh weather conditions. Shea had an open face that pointed directly to the water, delivering stinging winds that cut to the very heart of our solar-plexus – especially way up top in the upper level. The only way to stay warm was to either scream your head off for three hours, drink massive amounts of hot cocoa, or get stupid, cock-eyed drunk. Here's a list of places colder than the upper deck of Shea Stadium in winter. Antarctica… Siberia... The area where the Titanic sunk. End of list. We came prepared with blankets, booze and our lungs filled with rage.

Most of the men drank heartily from flasks and passed them around with glee. Drinking straight scotch for hours and screaming till purple in the face can leave one deliriously pieeyed. We had four choice seats next to the stairs about 15 rows down from the very top.

We knew immediately the games would be a constant source of entertainment. During an early season game, my father, who usually occupied the end seat next to the steep cement stairs, scampered off to the bathroom. He himself was probably a few beers in and had to relieve himself. Of course, he left when the Jets were driving towards the end zone and scored a rare touchdown. A guy in the very last row stood to cheer, lost his balance and fell into the guy in front of him – causing a bruising domino effect, which rumbled down the rows until the guy who was behind my father, came crashing face-first into my father's empty space, his face smacking harshly where my father's feet would have been. Because my Dad had left, he broke the chain of dominos causing an abrupt end to the fun. Another chain that was broken was the years that poor bastard who fell spent with his adult teeth. He left holding a pool of blood around his mouth and we never saw him again.

Tailgating has been around since the beginning of sports. Parking your car and roasting hot dogs while tossing a football around the parking lot is a joy that is hard to replicate. On more than one occasion, besides hot dogs being roasted in the parking lot, we had a few cars being roasted -- full-on raging fires till the car disintegrated into a charcoaled shell. This may be the result of many things, like someone leaving hot coals in their car, which sparked the flame. In 1980, every car was a tankard of cheap American parts and gasoline, which could catch fire as easily as tossing a match on dry kindling. Sometimes it was a result of partying gone crazy. After a particularly rousing game between the Miami Dolphins where

Richard Todd tossed a 75-yard bomb to Wesley Walker in the end zone for a last second win, we exited to a sea of smoking car fires that could be seen from space. How these people got home I'm not sure, but perhaps a good car fire celebration is something you do in the moment, tossing future consequences into the frozen wind.

One time we arrived at the parking lot to find a car already on fire. This couldn't have been charcoal embers or an unbridled celebration because it was early, and the day was just beginning. Not only that, the engine was on fire. Unless the guy was flipping burgers on the engine block, this was automobile malfunction. As we passed, the owner was standing on his front bumper, pissing on the engine, dousing the flames in good time as he disappeared in a cloud of white smoke. That's American ingenuity right there for you.

Very rarely did we park in the parking lot. There was limited space, so we were forced to park under random, darkened overpasses or in front of sketchy chop shops whose employees would lick their chops as they watched us leave. Somehow we never had a problem. On game day, Shea stadium was a sea of twisted traffic cones, hand written signs, and parking lot deals, but once the game was over and we returned to our car, it was usually sitting naked like someone had abandoned it after a drunken joyride. When it was enthusiastically parked next to a cluster of other game-going patrons, it all made sense, but after the game, it was leaning tilted on an embankment with the back half in the street.

The creepy parking situation and flaming cars already set a toxic precedent in my mother – an avowed fan of football. She came to exactly two Jets games in her lifetime. The first was the aforementioned face-plant game where the guy lost half his face. She basically spent the entire game on the bathroom line and saw perhaps 45seconds of game time. The second game, she was stuffed next to a man who could only be described as some kind of Minotaur. Not only did he smell terrible, but he cursed like a sailor till my mother's ears bled. My mother had been around the block once or twice too. We have a big, foul-mouthed family and they curse as good as anyone. But the man apparently displayed a level of cussing that for some would be considered an art-form, but to my mother, it rocked her to her Christian-raised core. After three hours of verbal vomit, the Minotaur ended his enchanting display by spilling a full beer on her. That was it. She was out. We never saw her at a game again. In her place was a steady flow of friends, cousins and uncles.

Rounding into form in 1981 was the second coming of the Jets glory years. Their stellar, legendary, bone-crushing defense. Massive Joe Klecko, Marty Lyons, Abdul Salaam and berserker Mark Gastineau, these titans laid waste to quarterbacks throughout the league. Along with high-flying safety Greg Buttle, the "New York Sack Exchange" crushed QBs to the tune of about five to six sacks a game. That is an almost unheard of stat if you look over the years of NFL defensive play. In 1982, Gastineau alone had 22.5 sacks, leading the league and setting a record that would stand for decades.

Mark would pound quarterbacks into the ground and do an arm-flailing, gladiatorial scream dance that would lather the crowd into an uncontrollable frenzy. Although I loved Gastineau with all my heart, I'm sure he, as well as half the league were operating on 50% blood steroid level. But the reciprocation of bonkers lunacy the crowd gave back to Gastineau after a sack could only be measured successfully on a Richter scale. The fans would scream and howl so viciously, my little head would rattle and I'm positive I saw people gnashing meat off long-bowed ribs like Vikings after a village plunder.

Preparing for a home game was a week-long event for me. It started Monday in school. Burning with the energy of Sunday's game, I'd commission my entire class to man the thee-hole paper punch – the squeaky black bar the teacher used to get tests and papers into binders. Friends would feed paper into the contraption and I'd hammer the punch down like a factory worker. Others would use the single-hole punch – the thing that looks like a hand-grip nail clipper. By weeks' end, we'd fill bags with all the circular chads punched from the paper that I'd use at the game as confetti. Any quarterback sack or touchdown scored, I'd run down to the end of the stairs, grip the railing and toss hand-fulls of confetti over the side. Depending on my excitement, sometimes I'd dump a whole bag into the air. Usually the blustery wind would blow the confetti back into my face and I'd turn to see my section snowed-over in paper chads. Fortunately, everyone was so hammered on whiskey, the crowd found my bouts of confetti explosions charming.

One of the many joys of attending a Jets game that delights Jets fans and annoys every other fanbase the league over… as well as fans of other sports including hockey, baseball and European football, is the acclaimed JETS chant. Rumored to have started in the late 1970s, the chant begins to swell with a bold, sometimes, intoxicated conductor who raises his hands to the rabid orchestra of fans, who fill their lungs to the brim and scream J-E-T-S Jets! Jets! Jets! in unison. It pumps the crowd into a tizzy and raises the level of play on the field... we perceive.

Having been led by the now infamous Fireman Ed for decades, during my heydays in Shea Stadium's upper level, this Jets cry was led by not one, but two band leaders – both who donned large afro wigs. The lunatic to our left wore a rainbow afro wig and the maniac who led our section wore a green afro wig. At some point, to up the hoopla level, our green-coifed conductor would accompany his J-E-T-S chant by physically spelling out the letters with his body. For the J, he'd turn to the side and curl his leg back.... for E, he'd thrust his arms and a single leg out... the T was arms raised horizontally... and for the masterstroke, the S was presented as a leg curl similar to the J, but with a swan-headed arm curl over his head to make a perfect S. The last three JETS, JETS, JETS were emphasized with fist pumps. Then he'd turn to his rainbow-haired comrade who'd work his section into a similar chorus.

As a wide-eyed and influential 10 year-old, these chants were the highlight of my game going adventures. Today, well... who am I kidding? They're *still* the highlight of my game going adventures! There's nothing like screaming as loud as you can until you lose your voice. It makes the people in your house happy because you'll be quiet for once.

In 1982, during a strike-shortened season, the Jets went to the AFC Championship and were defeated by the Miami Dolphins. The New York Sack Exchange continued their reign of terror on the league, but the tides were turning. As the years went on and the embers of the car fires dimmed, the Jets eventually left Shea Stadium for the browner pastures of The Meadowlands, New Jersey — a literal swamp that was cemented over because I assume they got the land for pennies on the dollar. 1983 would be the Jets last year in the frozen tundra of Shea and 1984 would start a whole new Jersey journey.

Ken O'Brien, a quarterback no one had ever heard of, including some of his own family members, was drafted to replace Richard Todd, and thus marked the beginning of futility that has haunted the franchise for a solid 40 years. Besides a never-ending series of baffling draft choices, befuddling free agent acquisitions, and bemused player development, the Jets have hired a parade of coaches and front office executives so incompetent, when they left the Jets organization they not only left football, they were never heard from in any capacity ever again.

In my long and humbling career as a Jets fans, I've gently folded and stored my Gastineau #99 Jersey in spirit-crushing defeat so many times, it's become a rite of passage marking my days from a glee-filled, bouncing boy – to grey-bearded, world-weary older man. But the storing away of the jersey is only superseded by the amount of times I've resurrected the jersey seven months later... when the season starts anew, the hope has been rehabilitated, and the brain has forgotten every terrible and deflating action that's happened before it. The roar of the crowd raises from mumble to gut-busting shout, and the coolers are filled with ice and beer in hopes of dulling the senses for the upcoming loses and bad decisions that have paralyzed our growth into positive and confident human beings.

I will stand confidently by my TV, or in the actual stands themselves, and prepare myself to shout along with my fellow fans in glorious unison to the Jets cheer. I will cheer regardless... whether it's a terrible play, or a touchdown. I will scream at the top of my lungs for all to hear. Because that's what we do.

The nature of fandom is irrational and extreme. Why do we choose the teams we choose? Because the team plays in our immediate area? Are we protecting our territory? Defending our land? My son likes the Carolina Panthers because he thought Panthers were cool. It's as simple as that. What more rationale does one need? My buddy Ned, who was born and raised in Colorado, roots for the Pittsburg Steelers because like me, he was watching Super Bowl XIV and made the wise decision to root for the Pittsburg Steelers. Another generation is coming up who'll root for The New England Patriots because they went to the Super Bowl nine times in 20 years, winning six of them. Those fans will be all over the United States and from other countries too – maybe Mars. The Dallas Cowboys recruited more fans in the early 1980s parading their hot-pants cheerleaders across the television than any Super Bowl win could have hoped to achieve. Sex doesn't just sell – it sinks its teeth into the depth of the human psyche.

Some fandom is passed down through generations. Walk into the living room of your Philadelphia home wearing a New York Giants jersey and you could be disinherited... or, at the very least, forever fighting over the mashed potatoes at contentious Thanksgiving dinners.

I've quit and returned to the New York Jets so many times, I've grown dizzy from the constant flip-flopping. Because, as Michael Corleone so eloquently states in *Godfather: Part III*: "just when I thought I was out, they pull me back in."

But, to try and stop fandom – or perhaps stop the love for a team when it's imbedded under the skin, is to lie to one's self. I can never quit them, so I'll continue to suffer. That's the decision I made back in 1980 on such a winter's day.

I wouldn't have it any other way.

A.J.'s Annual Interzone Super Bowl Party

For some reason, in the late part of the 19th and early part of the 20th century, people went by initials. D.A. Pennebaker, W.B. Mason, F.W. Murnau. Look at the cover of an old Saturday Evening Post and it's a list of initialed people. There are many famous and influential initialed people through time... W.C. Fields (wise-ass actor), B.B. King (Blues guitar legend), K.D. Lang (singer/songwriter) and Y.A. Tittle (quarterback for the Baltimore Colts, S.F. 49ers and the N.Y. Giants). Writers especially like to be initialed... J.K. Rowling, J.R.R. Tolkien, George R.R. Martin (N.Y. Jets Fan, BTW), A.A. Milne, W.E.B. Dubois and H.G. Wells... the list goes on.

I believe this was done to give an air of sophistication and mystery to one's persona. Unfortunately, whenever anyone asks me "what does A.J. stands for?" I tell them "Andrew Joseph" and their reaction is similar to a person whose balloon has deflated. I'm not sure what they were expecting -- probably some fascinatingly convoluted sequence of names that ended with fireworks and a key to the city. Granted, I've never been a huge fan of the name Andrew myself. It doesn't evoke a huge amount of joy nor anger... it's sort of right in the middle – like a slice of cheese. So I'm happy to go by A.J. as its own entity.

Andrew is a fine enough name, I suppose. Y.A. Tittle's name is Yelberton Abraham. Who in H-E-double-hockey-sticks names their kid Yelberton? Shockingly, Y.A. is a Junior, so his father was Yelberton too... Yelberton Abraham Tittle Senior. Big Yelberton liked his name so much he felt entitled to pass the name down. Little Yelberton probably didn't feel the same and went by initials. Y.A. became a football legend, but he never won a Super Bowl. In fact, he retired 3 years before the Super Bowl was invented.

My great grandfather was also one of those initialed people in the early 20th century. A.J. Schmitz the first, although he didn't go by A.J. Schmitz the first as that would be ridiculous. He had no lineage at the time. So he didn't walk around and say "I'm A.J. Schmitz the first!" He was just A.J. Schmitz (0 Super Bowls – excellent business man). At one point he was part owner of the Brooklyn Dodgers. His son, A.J. Jr. was a cornerstone in the building of Pfizer (the hard-on medicine people). My father, A.J. III, was a well-known architect on Long Island... and then there's me, the guy who wrote this book (rapid descent, I know).

I'm A.J. Schmitz IV. That's the number 4 for people who don't know Roman Numerals or Super Bowls. (The K.C. Chiefs won Super Bowl IV by the way). I don't go around saying I'm A.J. Schmitz the fourth like my great grandfather didn't go around saying he was A.J. Schmitz the first. *I do* call my son Maximilian Schmitz the first, though. The reason being is I want to make it clear to him that he can start his own numerical Max clan if he chooses to do so. I didn't want him to be A.J. Schmitz the fifth so I named him Maximilian. I put an end to that numerical madness. What are we – French kings? Once you go past the number 4 in the naming of people, you slide down a slippery slope. Where do you stop? 4 seems like a safe bet, but once you hit 5, there's immense pressure to keep it going. Like a human endurance challenge about how many olives you can stuff in your mouth at once. 40 seems like an absurd amount, but if you've got a fervent mob of people egging you on, there's no doubt you can push it to 50 and maybe beyond.

Sometimes when you fill out online forms, there's a dropdown for the suffix of your name. There's been a few occasions where IV was the last choice and a few times the last choice was V. Again, V being 5 in roman numerals. (In super bowl V, The Baltimore Colts defeated the Dallas Cowboys 16 to 13 in case you're wondering). So if you go beyond V, and name your kid VI (6), there's a good chance you've screwed them over and rendered them helpless to use the suffix drop down menu and properly fill-in their legal name. They may be filling out forms to buy a car or get a credit card and the next thing you know, they're living in the street. You tried to be vain about things and gave them a highfalutin suffix like VI, but you've doomed them to a life of perennial problems. So don't be that insufferable. Stop at IV or V.

Roman numeral IV and Roman numeral VI are very close to each other. There's been a few times where I couldn't remember where the 'I' went... before or after the 'V'. It's the same sensation you get when you leave a mall and can't quite remember where you parked your car. It's just another reason to stop the suffix at IV or V and not name your kid VI. (The Dallas Cowboys crushed the Miami Dolphins 24 to 3 in Super Bowl VI).

There's been a few famous A.J.s through the years. On the east coast of the USA, there's a bunch of appliance stores called P.C. Richards and Sons and their main CEO was A.J. Richards, the first-born son. Growing up, the most famous A.J. we all knew was A.J. Foyt, the famous race car driver. A.J. Foyt is a Jr. and his grandson is A.J. Foyt IV, who is quite ironically, a scout for the Indianapolis Colts. Go figure! (The Indianapolis Colts won Super Bowl XLI (41), defeating the Chicago Bears 29 to 17). I don't know if A.J. Foyt IV has a son that is a V, but if he does, we may need to have a conversation. We can chat when the Colts play the Jets.

Singer songwriter Jim Croce had a son named A.J.; A.J. Duhe was a linebacker for the Miami Dolphins (2 Super Bowls – both loses) and was a pain in the neck for the N.Y. Jets over the years. A.J. hawk was a consistent name in the modern football landscape. (A.J. Hawk won Super Bowl XLV (45) with the Green Bay Packers, defeating the Pittsburgh Steelers 31 to 25). Actress A.J. Langer popped up on the TV once in a while… most notably in the 90s hit show *My So Called Life* (0 Super Bowls).

If you Google A.J. Schmitz, a bunch pop up. I thought maybe A.J. Schmitz would be a fairly original name, but there's a slew of them. One guy even writes books! No, I'm not talking about *me*, I'm talking about A.J. Schmitz the novelist. I write *memoirs*. Maybe check out A.J. Schmitz the novelist. He could be good... I don't know. We share the same name and that's all. I don't advocate for him. But I don't want him to fail either.

There's lots of famous A.J.s, but we don't need to get into all of them... there's only so many hours in the day. I'm not a famous A.J. whatsoever. I may be famous by the time this book is printed, but I doubt it. (I've won no Super Bowls.)

There's also some famous fictional A.J.s as well. A.J. Raffles (created by E.W. Hornung – go figure), originally appeared in short stories and books around 1898. A.J. Raffles was a gentleman thief and safecracker. New Jersey's most famous gangster Tony Soprano had a troubled, underachieving and borderline stupid son named A.J. (first appearance in 1999) who did nothing but cause angina to both Tony, his wife Carmela and anyone named A.J. in real life.

But tucked in the fictional timeline in 1959, almost exactly 60 years after Raffles and 40 years before Soprano was a guy named A.J. in a sweet and tender little book called *Naked Lunch*, written by William S. Burroughs.

Norman Mailer stated that Burroughs was "the only American writer who may be conceivably possessed by genius." If Mailer came to that conclusion after reading *Naked Lunch*, I can only assume Norm was heavily doped on Morphine and read the text after a cavalcade of prepubescent choir boys coated his eyes with their spurting jizz when they jerked off a rainbow fountain over his head until his body writhed in peristalsis. If this seems like a bizarre and perverted descriptor, welcome to the world of *Naked Lunch*!

William S. Burroughs (0 Super Bowls – 1 "accidental" shooting of his wife in the head that killed her) was one of the famous Beat writers that came along in the 1950s and changed the way people read. The Beats prose tended to be an experimental, polarizing style that were heavily influenced by drugs, politics and social-issues.

Someone like, say, Jack Kerouac for instance, wrote... and some may say, *vomited* his words onto the page in a musical stream of consciousness – similar to Jazz. Kerouac, whose masterwork *On The Road* is a brilliant and sometimes exhausting series of debauched, cross-country treks, transports the reader to a time and place with his conversational style. Burroughs "masterwork" *Naked Lunch* is a series of endless bacchanals about exploding penises, spiked assholes, floor-shitting and drug-induced hallucinations that make little to no sense whatsoever. He wrote the book in the deep throes of heroin use and it's as twisted as it is depraved. These types of deranged and colored passages can be fun and inspiring in small doses – some of them brilliant and mesmerizing -- but reach the nearly 200 page mark of a book with neurotic, spasmodic, dripping-hose masturbatory smegma, and it begins to wear you down. It may also leave you to ponder why this type of thing is published and not the novel you wrote after a few beers by the fireplace.

I am by no means a prude. In fact, I'm a pervert champion. Get weird. I don't give a shit (on the floor or metaphorically). The *Naked Lunch* is a matter of personal taste. The book's influence has reached far and wide. I admit there are portions that ring like Jazz music. Some people hate Jazz music. I love it. The wonderfully eccentric hit machine (and Jazz-influenced) Steely Dan named their band after a steam-powered dildo in the book. Somehow, the brilliant director David Cronenberg made a film adaptation of the book, which is nothing like the book at all. Grunge legend Kurt Cobain recorded a spoken-word album with William Burroughs (Cobain died by gunshot to the head too – self-inflicted).

Burroughs was a homosexual and his writings are sort of a release of his pent-up sexuality that was tough to explore in the 1950s ("accidentally" shot his wife in the head, did he?). It's a psycho-sexual panorama of his desires, fueled by drugs and fever dreams. This type of thing wasn't around in the 1950s. It was pretty radical and that is obvious. Today it may appear as no more than a series of gilded, non-sequitur smut passages. Your acceptance of the material, historically or as diversion, may vary. But let's get back to the character of A.J.

First appearing in the chapter "Hassan's Rumpus Room," A.J. seems to be something of a troublemaker. Before he arrives, the scene is of a black-eyed insect Mugwump in pink silk, licking honey (My personal favorite cocktail) inside a Rococo bar. After the Mugwump strips a blond boy, ties his neck with red cord and cleans his ass with perfumed water because he's shit all over himself (I know, typical Saturday night for me too) he spikes the boy with his penis, which causes the boy to ejaculate. Mugwump then breaks the boy's neck from a gallows. After the boy shits again (this time cleanly which requires no cleaning) a green explosion occurs and everyone seems to have emptied their pipes.

Then a Satyr appears (again, typical Saturday night for me) and a black man impales a Chinese boy, who of course spurts sperm everywhere. Then a Javanese dancer impales a red-haired boy with his penis (a missed opportunity to call him a Javelin dancer) and then a Texan in a big 10-gallon hat shows up (don't ask) and all manner of young boys appear -- but not at the door as one might expect -- they come crashing from the ceiling, hanging and twitching by ropes from the neck. They consist of Arabs, Spanish, Mayans, Japanese and of course German youths who shout "Heil Hitler!" because... why not? (might as well go all the way!) More sperm shoots... I might as well preface that sperm shoots constantly, so I'll stop mentioning it. Assume every other line in this story is someone shooting a load of "rank-protein jizz" across a scene of colored iridescence and doing it immediately. (Apparently no on has the ability to hold back or control their Bulbocavernosus and Sphincter muscles).

So that those hanging boys are not left feeling alone, naked lifeguards enter with an iron lung of paralyzed youth who... well, need I say more? (sperm shooting... etc.) All of a sudden, Hassan shrieks "This is your doing A.J.! You poopa my party!" To which A.J. kindly retorts, "Uppa your ass, you liquefying gook!" and thus, A.J.'s sudden and definitive entrance into this tender story begins.

What Hassan is all up in arms (or cocks) about is unknown until a flood of "dripping cunt" lust-mad American women rush in and start viciously humping the boys (As you can see, this is an international story filled with universal acceptance of all kinds). A.J. begins shouting about "Sweitzers" and his personal secretary Mr. Hyslop (reading a comic book) informs A.J. the "Sweitzers" are "liquefied," which is met with a series of panic commands by A.J. until he grabs a cutlass and begins a rampage of beheadings on the women (again, typical Saturday night in my town). A.J. sings that "Yo, ho, ho and a bottle of rum" song as Hyslop raises the Jolly Roger (that's the skull and cross bones flag if you didn't know). A.J. squeals a Hog-Call and Eskimos flood the place and fuck the women, who I assume have no heads as A.J. has been beheading them.

The chapter ends with Hassan telling a cigar-smoking private eye (who's smashed his head through a wall, of course) that everything is "a filthy shambles!" Hassan then turns to see A.J., who is now dressed as a pirate, sitting on a sea chest drinking rum with a parrot and looking through one of those huge brass telescopes (Saturday night). Hassan berates A.J. calling him a "Cheap Fascist bitch!" and ends his tirade by stating conclusively to "never darken my rumpus room again!"

I know what you're thinking… "A.J. (Schmitz that is) surely you've partied this hard before" and the answer would be yes, I've partied pretty hard before, but I prefer to stick my penis into people who have heads on their shoulders (literally). Sure, I've screwed a few that didn't have heads on their shoulders figuratively, but that's another story. I also usually prefer sex with people whose necks are unbroken and not swinging from ropes. I also like them to have limbs and such. I mean, limbs that are missing because of previous shark attacks or other issues are fine… just not fresh bloody stumps from issues that happened minutes before I put my cock in them. I've sailed a few cum loads across a scenic view of dazzling lights, but everyone was of age, alive and consented to all acts.

I don't believe A.J. Raffles or A.J. Soprano had to

deal with things of this nature... so I move on to A.J. of *Naked Lunch.*

He appears again in a chapter of his own, this time titled: "A.J.'s Annual Party." Apparently he's the host of a party that, can you believe, is full of broken necks and spraying cocks! A.J. opens by calling his guests "cunts, pricks and fence straddlers." He draws our attention to a 60-foot red curtain that zaps open with lightning to reveal the Great Slashtubitch. After Slashtubitch boomerangs his monocle around the room, he starts a "Blue Movie," which in today's vernacular is called a porn video.

What starts as a young man and woman named Johnny and Mary gently petting, quickly devolves into her going to town on his anus with her mouth and eventually with a steam-powered dildo called Steely Dan III, which is Roman numerals for 3 (The New York Jets beat the Baltimore Colts in Super Bowl III, which I reference in the chapter before this in minor detail). Johnny spurts... well, you get it. He also questions what happened to Steely Dan I and II — I was torn up by a bull dyke, II was chewed by a baboon's asshole - or something. (Super Bowl I and II were both won by the Green Bay Packers, by the way).

Eventually a guy named Mark shows up... I'm going to spare you the details here. All I will say is, cocks spurt semen into the air, everyone's neck cracks like a dry twig, they swing from gallows, light themselves on fire and I believe a beagle shows up with a sheriff who inspects an ass and then a black man chases a "fag" down the hall. Everyone begs to be hung (again apparently – I don't know), which they are, then the lights come up and Johnny, Mary and Mark appear on stage with ropes around their neck and bow. Now thinking about it, although the chapter is called "A.J.'s Annual party," A.J. does not appear in it at all, really.

But, A.J. certainly appears later in a chapter titled: "Islam Incorporated and the Parties of Interzone." With a chapter seemingly focused on him, the narration goes from third person to first person, narrated by a guy who states A.J is an agent "like me" and A.J. may even represent a "trust of giant bugs from another galaxy." I made animated movies about giant bugs, so maybe A.J. and I have more in common than I think!

It's alluded that A.J. might be British, although as a supposed agent, he shows up disguised as a giant penis with a huge condom bearing his slogan "They Shall Not Pass" which I'm sure would get anyone made almost immediately. If truly British, James Bond would have tossed his martini. A.J. is referred to as "The Merchant of Sex" an "International Playboy" and a "Harmless Practical Joker" (all things I have not been called). One of A.J.'s great jokes was spiking a punch bowl at the US Embassy during a fourth of July celebration, which provoked a wild orgy (unfortunately this is fiction). Apparently Congress made him an official American. After a man insults him, A.J. retorts "Up yours with Interzone K.Y." a reference to the sex lubricant jelly.

One of A.J.'s great highlights is when he arrives at Chez Robert, a world-renowned restaurant, with six coked Bolivian Indians and proceeds to douse the gourmet food with ketchup (he really is American now). This stops the entire restaurant mid-chew, provoking Robert and staff to chase A.J. with broken bottles of '26 Brut champagne, meat cleavers and

Bowie knives. Tables overturn, food and wine crash to the floor and someone cries "Lynch Him!"

Being cornered, A.J. let's out one of his famous Hog-Calls, although this time it does not summon raping Eskimos but actual Hogs who slop the place and actually consume Robert who's had a stroke on the floor. The restaurant never recovers because Robert's brother Paul (who was in an insane asylum) takes over and starts to serve actual garbage and when A.J. tastes the food, declares it "garbage God damn it!" And insists Paul be cooked himself.

Later, "laughable, lovable, eccentric" A.J. appears in Venice, where he slices pigeons with a cutlass (really enjoys the cutlass), then boards his pink and blue barge donning giant velvet sails. Decked out in garish navy attire, he grabs the cock (shocking) of a gold statue, which squirts champagne into his mouth. He questions Mr. Hyslop (head buried in a comic book again) about where his "Nubians" are, which Mr. Hyslop declares are out "chasing cunt." A.J. insists Mr. Hyslop get the barge moving, and after a series of buttons are pressed, the barge rockets off, knocking over gondolas and crushing tourists until his vessel is sinking in the sea from a giant hole in the hull. A.J. shouts "Abandon ship, god damn it! Every man for himself!" as mambo music plays.

Suddenly, A.J.'s in Latin America at a school for delinquent boys. He's the M.C. of a statue unveiling. Tearing the giant cover away, he reveals a pink stone statue of boys (with flowers behind their ears) bending over each other with "flutes" and "bulges under cloth." Of course the statue is on top a limestone pyramid. A.J. christens the art by cracking champagne across the ass of one of the stone boys.

We whirl to the entrance of a Manhattan nightclub (my old stomping ground) where A.J. is pulling a purple-assed baboon by a gold chain. He tries to convince the manager the baboon is a poodle. One of A.J.'s entourage "stooges" proclaims that A.J. is "the last of the big time spenders" (again, something I've never been called) but that doesn't gain him entrance. At a club filled with "elegant fags and old cunts" A.J. stakes the baboon's leash to the floor. But after the baboon shits, A.J. whips the baboon's ass, who flies across the room and climbs on a woman who dies immediately from a heart attack. The baboon swings from the drapes and chandeliers and shits everywhere. A.J.'s stooges scold the baboon for "Upsetting A.J. after all he's done for you." A.J. screams that baboons are "Ingrates!" and ends his tirade stating that every one of them are ingrates… "Take it from an old queen."

That's pretty much where A.J. checks out of the story and the book. A reference to A.J.'s desire for the destruction of Israel is stated, but is most likely a "typical A.J. cover story." The rest of the chapter devolves into a drab list of Interzone and its twisted inhabitants. Thus ends the mysterious life of A.J. from *Naked Lunch.*

The (un)mysterious life of the real A.J. (me) will continue on. The only party that I plan to have that will get unruly will be the Super Bowl party I'll have when the N.Y. Jets finally make it to the big dance (won't hold my breath). I do have an annual Super Bowl party at my house, but it's usually fairly subdued because the teams involved are not my team. By night's end, we've analyzed the commercials, eaten mounds of chili (meat and veggie) and consumed large amounts of booze (no heroin).

When that fateful day comes and the Jets are in the Super bowl, I'm going to get one of those giant stadiums made of snack food. Maybe you've seen them. The crowd in the stands is an array of pretzel sticks, goldfish crackers (pizza and cheddar), potato chips, nachos and crackers. The field is a bog of onion and melted cheese dips, and the endzones are aligned with rows of hotdogs. If it's constructed by professional snack stadium builders, it should be edible from top to bottom. The guest list will be restricted to family and friends (No: baboons, shooting penises) who only pledge loyalty to the Jets.

I will sit back and contemplate the A.J.s of the world, whether they be fictitious or real. I'll dream of fame where A.J. Schmitz is a name everyone knows... but not the *other* A.J. Schmitz... although, there's room for two A.J. Schmitz's... maybe more! In my dream fantasy, I'll be interviewed by A.J. Hammer for some Entertainment Tonight segment... hopefully free of screaming, shitting, purple-assed baboons with pulsating cocks that explode jizz like leaping, kaleidoscopic dolphins. I don't believe that makes for good television. Maybe something on a streaming service, but I don't know.

As I daydream, I'll put "AJ Scratch" by Kurtis Blow on the stereo (AJ Scratch is a rap song about a D.J. from the Bronx). I'll put some football on the T.V. where I may see A.J. Brown (1 Super Bowl – a loss) of the Philadelphia Eagles catch a touchdown (hopefully not against the N.Y. Jets though). But if he catches one against the N.Y. Giants, S.F. 49ers or the L.A. Rams? That'd be O.K. by me.

DEATH AND TAXES

Benjamin Franklin said there are two things certain in life – death and taxes. I believe he was correct, although I'm not dead yet. Ben is dead, so he must have been correct. I've been taxed to death, although not literally.

The Beatles sang a song in 1967 called *Taxman* because they were so frustrated by the amount of taxes being heaped upon them from every little transaction they made. Heck, the United States seceded from England over taxes. We started a war and everything – where a lot of people died! That's how annoying taxes can be.

Both the Beatles and The United States were dealing with England who has notoriously high taxes, so maybe England is to blame for taxes… not only in England, but elsewhere.

There was a saying that "the sun never set in England" – a reference to the amount of land they occupied around the world at one point. The English navy sailed the 7 seas and planted a flag whenever they hit a shore. They implemented taxes, which drove every native to the brink of sanity, forcing them to take arms and revolt. Pretty much every piece of land England once owned around the globe turned against them and it mostly had to do with taxes.

I'm sure rape, slavery, religion and general misery brought on by England's ideology played a part too, but let's just say it was taxes.

What makes taxes so frustrating is that money can't move from one place to the other without it being taxed. If you took a pile of $100 bills and moved them from your kitchen to your dining room, you will be taxed. "Room Tax" they'll say, and stick out their greedy little paw for a cut of the pie.

There's income tax for both the federal and state government, city tax, property tax and even inheritance tax. If someone in your family dies and leaves you money, the government gets a cut. How that works, I'm not sure, but money goes from the dead person's bank account to yours and the government gets some.

I get it. The government doesn't run without taxes. They need trillions of dollars to run the jalopy. At least the United States does. The U.S. Government collects about 5 trillion dollars in taxes from its people every year and proceeds to spend about 8 trillion.

I know, the math doesn't add up!

That's why we're several trillion dollars in debt... and the tally keeps rising. By the time I'm dead, I'll owe something like $180,000 for my share of the debt. I'd like to see them try and collect on that. On my deathbed I'll send the government my bank statement and have a good laugh as my heart stops beating.

Once I'm in heaven, I can play worry-free ping pong with Ben Franklin and Jimi Hendrix. I can't be taxed in heaven... at least, I don't think I can. I've never been there. Heaven tax? I wouldn't rule it out.

Hell probably has no taxes. Satan seems like the kind of demon who is vehemently against taxes. But, Satan might damn your soul in others ways – like making you wait in your accountant's waiting room for eternity while the sound system endlessly plays The Beatles *Taxman* on kazoos.

More frustrating than the idea of taxes is doing taxes. Being an artist and a writer, I'm not exactly a whiz when it comes to economics, but I've freelanced almost my whole life and I've been forced to figure it out. I learned early on that the best way to do your taxes is to hire an accountant.

If I was to tell you for a measly $400 you could avoid weeks of misery and pain, you'd pay that cost; wouldn't you? $400 in this day and age will get you a quality accountant and they'll do your taxes for you -- absolving you the abject misery of figuring it out for yourself.

Years ago I helped my friend Tony do his taxes and after many late nights clutching receipts and drinking hard liquor, I knew what the future held for me. Hire an accountant. These people go to college for this shit. They know tax law! They know what they're doing... you don't!

A person who defends himself in a court of law has a fool for a client and the same goes for someone doing their own taxes. Defend yourself poorly in court and you could be going to jail where you're the boy toy of a 300-pound gorilla who spends half his day in the weight room. It's hard to escape the firm grasp of a strong man in a 10x10 cell. There's no place to hide. And for some reason, the guards give Vaseline to the inmates. It's not for ashy elbows, I can tell you that.

Stop paying your taxes altogether and you could be going to jail too. They don't toss you in general public with the crazy gang-bangers; but you don't want to take that chance. One paperwork snafu and you could be doing time with a guy who killed his entire office because the neighbor's cat told him to.

Get your taxes done.

My accountant's office is in the Empire State Building. I thought it'd be a high-class chic pad, but it looked like a giant broom closet. He had an old-fashioned iron spiral staircase in the middle of the floor leading downstairs. When I asked him where it led to, he couldn't be sure. He's an accountant, not a private detective. He does excellent work. I get my taxes done.

The strangest part about taxes is the constant negotiation process of it. Hypothetically, you owe the government a certain amount and then meticulously try and recover it by sifting through every transaction to squeeze some back. It's tedious.

It's another reason to hire an accountant. Going through every transaction you made over the course of 365 days is mind-numbing. Not only that, it gives you time to reflect on your poor choices as a consumer.

"We went to the ice cream shop 40 times last year?"

"Why did we spend eight grand on clothes?"

I wear a black t-shirt and jeans every day, so I'm not sure how we spent so much money on clothes. We can't afford to go anywhere in our new clothes because our dining money goes to taxes. My family could have worn potato sacks every day and no one would have noticed.

My wife likes to be fashionable for sure, but my son is growing like a weed. He wakes up every other day and needs a new pair of pants. We try and jam shoes on his feet like Cinderella. It'd be cheaper to wrap his feet in newspaper until he's 18 and save a few thousand dollars on shoes.

The government likes to nickel and dime us, but the tax negotiation process is nickel and diming them back. You can write off lots of expenses if you know where to look.

"Cheeseburger? Business expense."

Accountants know where to hunt for savings in the nooks and crannies. They'll find savings crannies where you didn't know there were nooks. But, it works for people who don't need to save money at all. Like millionaires… and especially billionaires.

While you're saving $1.17 on a laptop computer you got last summer, a rich hog is getting $1.7 million on a computer firm they purchased last summer.

"You bought an oil refinery last summer? The government should be paying YOU, my friend."

A tax return is like playing roulette. The wheel spins and you wring your hands to see if you hit pay dirt. If the little ball hits your number, you're getting paid. If not, the house takes your cash. I send my taxes off and stress-out for a month.

Tax returns can really have a big plus or minus swing. Getting $1,000 back is pretty good, but paying $1,000? It's devastating! That's a two grand swing! I can't afford that, and most people can't. You go from eating ice cream in your new sneakers to eating beans in a potato sack in one fell swoop.

One year I had to pay $10,000 in back taxes and I almost had a coronary. But the following year I got $5,000 in refunds. I don't know. Are we sure we're doing this thing correctly? Seems off to me.

Worse than having to pay more taxes than expected is being audited. That's when the government thinks you've been lying about your taxes and storms in to check it out for themselves. I've never been audited, but I fully expect to be the second this book hits the shelves. I'm playing with karma here. Murphy's Law. The second you say "I've never broken a bone" is the second you crumble down a flight of concrete stairs.

If the government wants to audit me, more power to them. They're welcome to come and sift through every rumpled scrap of paper that I've been tossing into moldy cardboard boxes in my attic. And I've truly kept them all! If I've purchased even a single piece of chewing gum in the last 20 years, I've kept the receipt. My life is in shambles... clothes strewn across the floor and mail unopened... but I've kept meticulous track of my spending.

The Government accountant can hunker down at my kitchen table with a calculator, three gallons of coffee and a 12 pack of Claritin and comb through every fungus-y fragment that's cranked through a cash register for the last 7 years.

Hopefully they don't find any glaring issues, because... gorilla, Vaseline... etc.

I'm not really cut out for prison. I bruise easily and

I don't need a boyfriend. I have enough emotional baggage right now. Looking through my receipts, I've spent enough on gift items for two families. I don't need to send a valentine to my prison bunk-mate once I'm released.

Many people are God-fearing people but I'm a government fearing person. That's probably why my taxes are buttoned up tight. The last thing I need is the government in my business. They can barely take care of themselves, let alone me. I've seen enough bad movies to know that the government's incredible stupidity and endless stream of red tape can bury an innocent person into oblivion.

For years, people have been clamoring for schools to teach their kids useful things like banking and taxes. Kids should know early on in life how depressing taxes are, which may backfire as it may dissuade them from leaving the house to face the real world.

We can eliminate some subjects like trigonometry to make room for tax classes. I mean, who uses trigonometry in the real world? I barely use addition and subtraction. Trig is for people flying large airships to the outer rims of our solar system. I'm sure substituting a tax class for one of the 67 math classes my son takes will not harm him.

If a gasket blows on the engine of a space shuttle upon takeoff, we can look to the eggheads who paid attention to trigonometry in school and not to my son who took a tax class.

It's not a coincidence that Ben Franklin is on the $100 bill. He's the symbol of money and taxes. That's why it's all about the Benjamins. They're either coming or going from your bank account.

GROCERY SCORE

When I say I'm running to the supermarket, I mean literally… at top speed.

I treat a trip to the grocery store like a hostage rescue. I try and get in and out before anyone knows what the hell is going on. If I had smoke grenades it would make the process easier, but I believe that type of thing is frowned upon in the produce section.

Grocery shopping is high on my list of things I despise. Unfortunately, I need to do it often because as it's well known, we stupid humans need to eat about 15 times a day. It's a flaw in our design. Apparently it has something to do with our brains and how much energy and sugar they use. They generate a massive amount of heat, so the computer swimming around in our skull needs a constant stream of fuel. Or something like that. My Romanian friend Alex, who's a doctor, told me this while eating a raw onion like Bugs Bunny chomping a carrot. The information entered my brain in various waves of fascination and disgust as the crunching and chewing of the onion overtook my senses.

I believe Romania is a country touched by the Industrial Revolution so they have fire and stoves and cooking utensils so they don't have to eat raw onions. But who am I to judge? I was born and raised in a country that will serve a full breakfast of bacon, eggs and hash-browns on a hamburger that is already dripping with three kinds of cheese.

Considering how fat the planet has gotten in the past 30 years, I have no doubt that our need for constant food consumption has less to do with our brain, and more to do with our giant, fat asses. Or more specifically, our will power. If you watch sports, you'll notice that the average athlete has doubled in size. Some of that is performance-enhancing drugs. Some of it is competition. If the arms of the guy on the other team are twice the size of yours, and he's jacking baseballs further than a scud missile, you may want to up your game as well.

I have been blessed, so I'm told, by having the problem of not being fat enough. I have the metabolism of a humming bird and burn through fuel faster than a Hummer. I'm constantly eating, which can be annoying for the people living in my home because there's a constant rustling in the pantry and crunching in their ears. Because of my metabolism, I believe I'll die early. They say a candle that burns twice as bright, lasts half as long and if that's the case, I could drop in the middle of this sentence. But I need a constant source of food, which requires frequent trips to the supermarket.

I'm vehemently opposed to the "big shop" like people

do at Costco and large haul shopping places of their ilk. Living in Manhattan for years, I'd stroll home and pick up what I needed for the day. It was the beauty of city living. In the 'burbs, you try and stock your shelves like it's Armageddon. You fill your giant cart with a 50-pound crate of peanut butter, then catch your reflection in the freezer door, which forces you to contemplate your terrible life choices. I suppose if you have 8 kids, these places make sense. You're there every week as your 5 sons, who all play sports, are gobbling up the inventory at an alarming rate. The Costco I once visited had barbed-wire around a section of gated metal fencing. If you genuinely want to feel like you're in the middle of the apocalypse, buy a six-pack of Advil under a snaking coil of razor-wire that will slice every major organ in your body like boloney. Don't be surprised if you encounter a Mohawk-ed man on a motorcycle sizing up your skin to make a full body-suit when it's every man for himself in the mob panic.

Because I refuse to do the big shop even at my local, sensibly-sized grocery store, I'm in a constant state of *hitting* the supermarket. Depending on what I need, I attack it with a hard thought plan. Sometimes I'll even draw a map with boxes that indicate sections, potential traps and landmines. I don't want to 'double-back' and hit a section I've already left. For me, once I've left the produce department, I don't want to return under any circumstances. It feels like a failure of the mission if I have to return to the scene of the crime once I've escaped scot-free.

"Shit, I forgot oranges!"

"You can't go back! It's too late!"

"But goddamn it, my wife likes oranges!"

"I'm sorry, A.J. You simply have to move on!"

I gaze back at the oranges in frustration as I enter the cheese section… like I'm leaving a prisoner of war behind as our chopper lifts into the air. I squeeze a tear from my eye and hold my hand out longingly as I slowly enter the meat department. I could have gotten those oranges… if I just had one more chance!

Later, I tell my wife that they were out of oranges. She asks *why* and I tell her *I don't know*. Why she thinks I would know what happened to the orange supply is beyond me. Perhaps she thinks I'm talking to the people in the fruit area and grilling them as to what happened to the oranges -- like *they* would know. My wife will ask me if I asked the staff if they know what happened to the oranges and I say "of course not!" Why would they have the shipping knowledge of oranges, or broccoli, or knowledge of anything in the world other than the *likes* on their social media feeds? These people hate their jobs. Somehow they're able to stock the shelves with one hand while the other hand is scrolling through their phones. Pretty much every person at the store is one-handed and doing their job with a look of anguish.

Sometimes when I forget something, I'll tell my wife a fabricated story about how there was a massive orange truck disaster on the Florida freeway and she shakes her head in dismay. It gets her off my back and resolves me of responsibility. Sometimes I'll forget a bunch of items and have to come up with some fast excuses on the spot.

"Where's the salad?"

"Bad fungus in California"

"Did you get sugar?"

"Supply chain issues."

"Milk?"

"They were out."

"Yogurt?"

"Yeast shortage."

"Ice cream?"

"The freezer was broken."

"Dish soap?"

"I thought we had some!"

"Flour?"

"I thought you meant flowers and they didn't look healthy."

"Tea?"

"It was on sale and everything was gone."

"Chicken?"

"Bird flu."

Unfortunately, I'm running out of excuses. I still have a good back-up list like "They were crushed" and a few nuggets to use on every occasion like "They weren't fresh." But at some point it becomes improv acting and I need to work on the fly.

My map planning is very tight and has me hit every section efficiently and with excellent timing. Sometimes I go first thing in the morning when the supermarket is empty. Of course I'll try and grab some chicken wings and the only other person in the entire store besides me is an 80 year-old lady and she's idling in front of the chicken wings with her cart -- taking up the entire section. I try and be patient, but she seems intent to check the size, weight, freshness date and coloring of all 75 packages in the section. It's summer, but she's wearing a scarf and cardigan and she's prepared to get the best deal imaginable on a pack of wings. I have empathy. She's on a fixed budget and needs to shop wisely, but the clock is ticking on the imaginary bomb-timer I've set in my head and it's tick-tick-ticking away. The frozen air does nothing to hinder her as she's probably encased in layers of wool. I say "excuse me" but her ears stopped working years ago and her ability to sense her surroundings is permanently set to 'I don't give a shit.' So I dodge around her, extend my arm as long as it can go and snatch a pack of wings and leave. It doesn't matter what the wings look like. I'm going to toss them on the grill and heat them till they're charred stumps, so the color and freshness is of little concern to me.

It's like the time I went to Bed bath and Beyond to get a spatula and the store was completely empty, devoid even of employees and when I got to the spatulas, a woman was standing there looking at spatulas. I don't know what you call that – Synchronicity? Murphy's Law? The place is the size of an airline hangar and she could have gone there for ANYTHING… a Keurig machine, pillows… wedding registry crystal goblets, but no… she's there for freakin' spatulas.

There's always something that hinders my grocery mission. Usually it's the stock boys who've wheeled an absurdly large cart of boxes and are crouched down stuffing things on the shelves. They've left an area big enough for an anorexic to pass through and no one else. I flat out refuse to go shopping on a Sunday where the place is jammed to the walls with families and their carts piled up to the ceiling. I go on Tuesday, after the smoke clears and the staff has had a full day of rest after drinking themselves into a stupor to forget the Sunday madness. But, Tuesday is usually restock day and that's a different level of madness. It means I'll be coming back on Wednesday and probably Friday as well. Maybe Saturday too. But I'd rather run in and out in 7 minutes than do a full 45 minutes on Sunday. Sunday is a holy day for me. It's when I watch football and basketball and anything else that's on the TV and doing anything besides going to the grocery store.

Once in a while I'll go to the fancy expensive market right down the street. It's a premium market because the food is expensive, but they have five checkout stations with people manning them at all times. It's a time vs. money issue. You'll spend $40 more for basic items, but you'll be in and out in seconds and back home doing important things like shredding the pile of junk mail the world seems determined to deliver daily.

Sometimes my map plans go south depending on the store layout. The condiment section doesn't have taco sauce. The taco sauce is in the same aisle as the beans, rice, pasta and other "international" foods. That can throw a mission off completely and a double-back is completely necessary. During the 2020 pandemic, I asked the stock boy where the taco sauce was located and he said there was a taco sauce shortage. It took all my strength to keep from gasping. Milk, bread, cheese, meat... you can toss all that shit right out the window, but when a staple like taco sauce is running low, you know things are going downhill. The worst is when I'm in strange territory – like on vacation or the next town over and the grocery store layout is completely different. I spend most of my time wondering what moron made *these* layout choices like putting the jelly and the bread on the opposite sides of the store. That's when you toss your map on the floor and use your instincts. Go rouge. Read the overhead signage.

Other things that can hinder a mission is a cart with a bum wheel. If you grab one and the 4th wheel is shot, you abandon it like a flat-tired Hummer and try to hotwire the next one. If that one has a bum wheel, you abandon the carts altogether. Go on foot. Of course if you're grabbing a cart, you're planning on a deep immersion behind enemy lines. You're going undercover as a responsible and sensible shopper and could be there for hours. You'll need patience, timing and practice the art of blending into your surroundings. You'll need to read labels and use the bottom rack of the cart for sacks of rice and crates of bottled liquids.

I visit many different markets because they have different things I like. One for meat, one for produce... one for dry goods. It's exhausting. That forces me to create a larger map of my town and hit them all at the right stages so the last stop is closest to home. One particular market has a price gun where you can scan the items as you place them in the cart. Not only does it give you the satisfaction of gripping a weapon, but you can pay and go at the end. Unfortunately the price guns never works correctly and much like the cart, I abandon it immediately... like a spent Glock... I toss it on top of melons, in the coffee aisle, or jam it into a rack of nuts.

I have different levels of attack at the supermarket. Sometimes I approach it like a jewel heist. I slip in gracefully and slide things off the shelf and into my bag like a cat burglar. I slink around endcaps and cereal displays as light-footed as a panther and slide through the self-checkout without being seen. Sometimes I hit it like Jim Brown in *The Dirty Dozen*. If you've never seen the film, The Dirty Dozen are a rag-tag crew of death-row inmates turned soldiers who secretly go behind German lines to kill a bunch of Nazi generals in a castle. At one point, Jim Brown takes a bunch of grenades and bolts through a promenade, dropping them into airshafts like greased lightning and is out before the first grenade blows. I hit the grocery store the same way. I literally run through and grab things off the shelf like a maniac and try and escape before the checkout lane is clogged with people. Shoppers stare at me like I'm psychotic and I leave nothing but wind in their hair as I dart by with an armful of potatoes.

Sometimes it's a group mission with family or friends. I reference the map and give people a section to conquer. Our mission: get what we need and get the hell out before trouble starts.

"You get the milk and butter."

"You find the chips."

"You get the beer. Try and get a lager and an IPA."

Other times, when alone, I approach it like a serene walk on the beach. I succumb to the madness and let the tranquility of the experience take me for a ride. I focus on the music, which has gotten better these days. It's usually a calm ditty like *Something So Strong* by Crowded House, or even a hip shaker like *The Sign* by Ace of Base. Back in the day, the grocery store sound system played creepy elevator music called Muzak. The playlist consisted of current radio hits played with soft orchestral arrangements that could lull any barking, mouth-frothing lunatic into deep and tranquil passivity. Nowadays, you can tap your foot to Bruce Hornsby and

Elton John while plowing rows of canned corn into your cart with your arm.

One time I ran into my friend Josh who was walking the aisle like a man who was shot by a tranquilizer gun. He was brushing over the shelf contents with his fingers – raking the labels like one might do with the sands of a Japanese garden. As I was zipping through in a furry, we stopped to chat.

"This is my Zen place" he confessed.

This is a man who has twins, so I understood completely. For him, the grocery store was the polar opposite for me. It was his escape. His place to organize his thoughts and categorize his feelings. Where I found the grocery store to be a cold and harsh environment where dreams go to die, he found warmth and inspiration where dreams can be rediscovered. As we parted, both with a smile, I knew I'd be out in minutes, where he was happy to spend the better part of the day.

Sometimes a slow stroll can help you discover food items… go off the game plan and hit the food markets… mingle with the locals. You'll discover whole roasted chickens, bready sandwiches, and deli salads with oily sheens usually found only in canopied, misty forests. My market has a sushi chef. I don't think this guy grew up thinking he'd be rolling sushi at the grocery store, but I suppose all dreams begin somewhere. In a year he could be opening his own restaurant while I'm still running through the place like a man on fire.

Of course no matter how fast or efficient your shopping game is, you fall prey to the one thing that can kill your mission. The check-out lane.

If you go to the self-checkout you'll invariably get

stuck because the cyborg machine won't recognize an item, or it doesn't understand the weight and thinks you're trying to rip-off the store by shaving an ounce off a head of cabbage. The overhead light will blink and you'll have to wait for the attendant to come and fix the situation. It's kind of like the airport attendant that's checking your passport as you're about to board the plane, having nearly gotten out of the country with the stolen gem as the local authorities are barreling down the corridor with guns and dogs.

The check-out attendant is knocking buttons with their knuckles... your mental clock ticking while you're holding your next scannable item. You've got the barcode exposed and you're ready to swipe. The attendant goes through three levels of authentication until the screen is clear and you can continue your mission and onto the plane.

You wave goodbye to the other customers as you exit with your sack of treasure. Their envy is palpable because the check-out computer will surely malfunction for them and slow their lofty goals of escaping the supermarket.

If you go through the normal checkout lane, you'll be at the mercy of not just the listless checkout person, but any and all civilians in the line of fire.

There's a number that morally requires you to go to the regular checkout line cattle chute.

That number is 12.

11 is *just* enough to sneak into the 10 items or less line, but 10 items is too much for self-checkout, so if you go 12 or up, you *have* to hit the regular checkout lane.

As sure as there are death and taxes, there's only going to be ONE checkout lane open, and you're forced to enter the death march behind the woman who's stocking a month's worth of food for her brood, an old man who moves like he's stuck in molasses, and the checkout lady's friend who thinks the check-out line is the *perfect* place to catch up after a decade apart.

The checkout lady's friend is the worst. You don't think anything of it at first because the checkout woman's friend is wearing sunglasses and flipping through a trashy tabloid magazine featuring a news story about how a super sexy celebrity now looks like someone with a case of flesh-eating bacteria. But then, like a master of disguise, she sheds her cold exterior and is a glistening ray of sunshine.

"How's everything? Stan is good? Prostate swollen like a grapefruit?"

She's more engaged than a talk therapist and hangs on every word the checkout lady mutters – all while ignoring the task of bagging her own groceries. The checkout lady talks animatedly while using a box of frozen waffles as a pointer – feigning the act of placing it into the bag as she continues to use it as a pointer to emphasize her point that gas prices are crazy and her back is killing her.

Once I get to the checkout, I layout my bags and shake my hands vigorously, like I'm waiting for wire cutters so I can dismantle the bomb. The checkout lady can't swipe fast enough. I gave her a stern "hello" to let her know I mean *all business*.

Once I got there, another check-out lane opened and the lady at the end of my line with five items has checked out and is exiting the parking lot already. I can see her in her Honda, happily leaving this warzone while I'm still bagging and stacking my items like a game of Tetris. I need to get all this crap into two ratty bags and carry it out with two hands or the mission is a complete failure.

I tap the card payment and scram. As I turn, the checkout person halts me and stuffs worthless coupons into my hand. I say worthless because I've never once in my entire life remembered to use a coupon. On the very rare occasion when I do bring a coupon, I only remember the coupon hours later after I remove my wallet and find it rumpled in my pocket – mangled and unused. After you've done this a few dozen times you give up on coupons.

The receipt at the end of the transaction is like a tally of bounty hunting scalps. The mission is complete and I'm on my way. Sometimes the checkout lady points out how much I saved that day and it's irrelevant to how much time I've saved by blazing through the place as if powered by rockets on roller skates.

The last stand is getting through the parking lot, dodging stray shopping carts and unaccompanied children without being mauled by an octogenarian who can't see over the steering wheel of their 1989 Lincoln Continental.

10-4

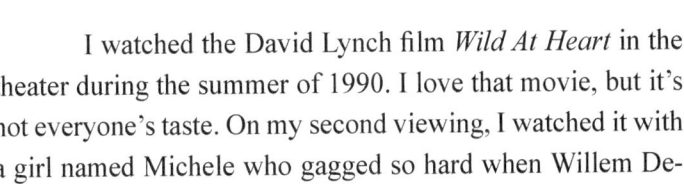

I watched the David Lynch film *Wild At Heart* in the theater during the summer of 1990. I love that movie, but it's not everyone's taste. On my second viewing, I watched it with a girl named Michele who gagged so hard when Willem Defoe accidentally blows his head off with a shotgun, she had to run to the bathroom because her gag reflex broke and she was going to hurl.

When I originally watched the film, there were about 10 people in the theater, including my girlfriend and me. It wasn't exactly a blockbuster hit. There's a scene where Nicolas Cage and Laura Dern are driving down the highway at night... top down on their convertible Ford Thunderbird ... wind blowing through their hair. There's a hypnotic guitar instrumental playing over the scene. I fell in love with that tune, so the next day I went to the music store in my town called *Soundtracks* to track it down.

Standing before the manager -- a young guy with a

Morrissey face, pompadour and swagger, I asked him if he knew the song.

"How did it go?" he asked.

I proceeded, like an idiot, to play the guitar twang from memory. But of course I didn't have a guitar, so I played the song with my mouth – making bizarre, warbling noises to mimic what can be denoted as a slide guitar.

"Bowww, Booooooooowww.... weww, weww, weww, weewwwwwww...."

As I was doing this, the older owner came from the back room with a younger woman in tow – their eyes glazed over like corn farmers who'd worked the land too long. The three of them stared at me like I had four heads. Perhaps my rendition was so mesmerizing, it invoked memories of days past, or a porn movie they recently enjoyed.

"Something like that." I said concluding my piece.

After they blinked about fifteen times, Morrissey turned towards the store's inner belly and said, "Yea, I think I remember that."

After he said that, I remembered that the three *Soundtracks* people were some of the people in the theater when I watched the film, sitting in a cluster a few rows ahead of me.

"That's right, you were at the movie last night." I said.

Morrissey shot me a look as if I'd violated his sanctity in some way. His eyes combed over me to see if I was recognizable in any way, shape or form. Considering he was in a group of eight people and I was in a group of two about five rows behind him to make up the total 10 in the audience,

I didn't think it was so hard to recall. I was a skinny pole with a shock of spiky, blond hair – like a cockatoo. Easy to notice in a dim, empty theater. But, I'm a fairly observant person. If I'm in an empty theater and I see a few people there, I notice them. I mark their faces, notice their flaws: pock marks, thrift shop bowling shirts, Morrissey pompadours. Things like that. But, he seemed oblivious to my existence.

"Yea, that's probably going to be on the film soundtrack, but we didn't get any yet." Morrissey revealed.

I left the store having not only embarrassed myself with mouth warbles, but also procured no music to listen to. I received a call a few days later from *Soundtracks* to let me know the *Wild At Heart* soundtrack was in. I immediately bought it. That song was the instrumental version of *Wicked Game* by Chris Isaak, by the way.

In today's modern world, that embarrassing performance I gave in *Soundtracks* could have been avoided completely. The Internet would have told me what that guitar song was in minutes. I could have downloaded the song and been listening to it in seconds. I wouldn't even need to put pants on. That's the beauty of the Internet. No pants. Many people don't wear pants while using the Internet, but that's for other reasons.

I'm not sure the Internet was even in our lexicon when I did that guitar performance. I'd be introduced to 'The Net' in about two years when my college roommate Pete, who was studying aerospace engineering, had to connect to the Internet to complete school assignments. He would place our shared home phone receiver on a cradle that connected him to the drab and boring Internet that consisted of nothing but numbers, letters and code. Long before we sent pictures of naked people and enjoyed horrifying videos of people dying in car accidents.

We always knew when Pete was doing homework because we'd pick up the kitchen phone to call a buddy for beers and were met with a series of jarring squeals and honks as well as the inevitable howl that Pete shouted from his bedroom after being disconnected. We probably cost Pete hours of quality work, or most likely, erased a safety measure on a jet plane he was designing that millions of people fly on every day because we wanted to connect with our friends and get hammered at Chuck's, a local bar that served underage students as care-free as McDonald's served chicken nuggets.

Before the Internet, it's hard to imagine how people did much of anything. Today, when you pay with a credit card, you know within seconds if your payment was approved or not. When I was a kid, you gave your credit card to a cashier, who would place it on a metal imprinter, then put carbon paper over it and crush it with a roller. Everything was reproduced in triplicate. It took about 45 minutes for the transaction to take place. If you thought people were impatient today, imagine back in 1984. Everything took three times as long. Credit was built on the honor system, which is the reason so many people passed bad checks. People would write checks at the grocery store for all their food while the cashier waited impatiently and told them the day's date. Companies wouldn't know a check bounced until a week later, when that person was comfortably sitting on a beach in a third-world tropical country, avoiding the law in plain sight.

If you wanted to communicate with creepy strangers before chat rooms were invented, there were only a few outlets at your disposal. You could be a pen pal with a stranger and write letters to them. Magazines advertised for Pen Pals or you could find a list at your local library. For closer contact with strangers, you could cruise the underground bars of darkened cities and meet perverts like yourself, or potentially an eager serial killer. Or you could do what I did to communicate with the strange and bizarre world outside my front door... get a CB radio.

Citizen Band radios were all the rage in the 70s and early 80s. The police and fire fighters of your town still use them today. For some reason, they were a big deal where I lived. Some of that popularity rose from *Smokey and The Bandit* starring Burt Reynolds.

The *Bandit* of the film, played by the charming, winking, million-watt smiled Reynolds, communicated to his trucker friend *Snowman* via CB, who was trucking Coors Beer across state lines. The popularity of CB in my town likely stemmed from the large fishing community that populated the waters of the bay. Good communication is a must when you're out on the water – clamming, checking lobster traps or snorting rails of cocaine while sunning with the gang.

My first CB was given to me by my neighbor Regina who had just upgraded. It was actually a car CB radio, but it worked fine as an intro. It wasn't as powerful as a desktop model... kind of like our current desktop to laptop computer ratio. Eventually, I upgraded with a desk model that my father got me at Radio Shack, America's finest electronics store named after a decrepit wooden hut you'd find rotting in your backyard. My father installed a giant antenna on our roof that he made out of thin aluminum tubing. It gave me ultimate range and the power to communicate with any white trash pedophile cruising around looking for a good time. With hundreds of channels to choose from, I could scan the airwaves in hopes of catching a deep conversation, a whisper of espionage, or a cry for help.

Of utmost importance when venturing into the enigmatic world of CB radio communication is to get a solid Handle. That's your name. Like *Bandit* and *Snowman*, mine was *Golden Eagle*. I'd sit in front of the CB on sweltering summer nights, twisting the dial as the red digital numbers flipped like a clock. I hunted for signs of life and called out for a "radio checks." That's when someone would hear you on the radio and reply back.

"Check one, check one, two. This is Golden Eagle looking for a radio check. Over."

Usually the response was a lonely trucker passing through, delivering frozen goods or hauling wood. They'd tell you their location… usually not further than the tri-state area… and where they were going. Once in a while they'd ask me for a good restaurant recommendation on Interstate 80, which was as useful as asking me where to score meth-amphetamine.

Even though we lived next door and could easily knock on each other's front door, Regina and I spoke nightly. Of the many highlights, we'd talk on channel 3, then tell the other to move to channel 33. We'd both radio check on 33, then talk there. Very exciting stuff. Sometimes that was necessary when some drunk was pestering us by shouting into the radio, forcing us to switch channels. Another highlight was when a fisherman reported to the police that he barbed a fish-hook through his eyeball and needed immediate help.

After many days twisting the squelch and clarifier knobs, searching for signs of life out in the quiet breeches of radioland's megahertz highway, Regina and I came across a guy in our town with the handle Star Trek. He was enthusiastic and had a goofy sense of humor. He was 19. At least, that's what he told us. I was 11 and Regina was 16, but it seemed perfectly acceptable to meet him at the local King Kullen grocery store parking lot.

A person named Star Trek imbues a particular image in one's mind. This was long before *Star Trek: The Next Generation*, or *Star Trek: Deep Space Nine*, or any of the other 50 incarnations to hit the TV over the years. At that point we'd only reached *Wrath of Khan* in the lexicon, the second film in the franchise. So the cult of the original show, which took life in TV syndication, was the fuel that boosted its fan's thrusters. The common image *Star Trek* invoked in everyone's mind of a nerdy, dripping, poorly groomed spaz was not a cliché, but usually right on target.

Star Trek *the person* did not disappoint.

When my sister Caroline found out that Regina and I were meeting a strange guy we met on the CB radio, she felt it was her duty to come and protect us. The three of us beamed into town and while baking in the summer heat of King Kullen's brutal black top parking lot, a tall, gangly guy rounded from behind a dumpster to greet us. Standing at about six foot two, Star Trek's red, zit-covered face was only dwarfed by his sun-bleached mullet – a flowering top of red spikes, off-set by a low-hanging set of nape drapes, which were the color of mud.

After some light banter, we asked Star Trek where he lived. He pointed behind the dumpster and said, "behind the grocery store." Regina laughed and said "Up the hill there?" indicating that maybe he resided in one of the many rows of houses that could be seen along the ridge.

"Yea," he said with a goofy grin. "Something like that."

It wasn't an answer we accepted with complete confidence. We decided to walk to the bowling alley in the middle of town, which ironically today, is a grocery store. We dropped quarters in the video game arcade while bowlers smoked cigarettes like chimneys and took full advantage of the building's air conditioning system.

While inflating dragons till they burst in the enchanted underground video game world of *Dig Dug*, My sister grabbed my arm and yanked me away.

"We're getting out of here." She demanded.

I didn't even need to ask. We bolted into the blinding sun and left Star Trek in the last frontier. Star Trek had asked Caroline out on a date and was getting a little too friendly, according to her, for someone we'd only met face-to-face 30 minutes before. Caroline wisely asked Star Trek to buy her a soda and took advantage of his cross-eyed gaze staring elsewhere for a chance to flee.

Back on our CB radios, Regina and I jumped around the dial, avoiding Star Trek like a Klingon Bird of Prey. Eventually we needed to talk with him and tell him that it wasn't going to work out. We were *Star Wars* fans… and underage. Regina told him to "get a life" and that was that. A harsh reality for Star Trek, but one that most likely catapulted him into a NASA scientist internship – or perhaps, a life of downtrodden misery where he elevated his social standing to nothing more than the dumpster of a better food distribution parking lot.

As the years went by, our CB radios disappeared from our desktops. The CB antenna on our roof was repurposed as our radio antennae. The connectivity we enjoyed through our CB radios was replaced with other forms of association. The old standby the telephone… sex with other human beings… and eventually, the Internet.

Today, you want to avoid people that look like Star Trek. Although if you're flipping through dating profiles online, it's possible you're looking at a man as handsome as Chris Pratt, but in reality, it's a guy that looks like Star Trek. Or perhaps, even worse – a guy that looks like Jabba the Hutt, or a Klingon of some sort. The mysterious anonymity of the Internet is no different than the dark cover of the CB radio.

My father still says "10-4" to people before he hangs up the phone, mixing up two forms of ancient communication sign-off. 10-4 in CB parlance means 'OK, message received.' But he seems to think it means goodbye.

To truly say "goodbye" to someone -- a trucker hauling beer, a pimple-faced dork, or to the entire communication process itself, you have to say "Over and Out."

THE 11 O'CLOCK "NEWS"

Does anyone watch the 11 O'clock news anymore? I can't image why they would if they do. In a world where we have the Internet, 24/7 news television and news apps, watching the 11 O'clock evening news is the equivalent of reading a newspaper (which is somehow still not dead) from 1982. It's completely irrelevant.

Watching these steely-eyed newscasters deliver the news in their detached, robotic voices is enough to curdle the soul. Their hair is gelled into place like cement and their pantsuits have not one crease in them... much like their skin. They tap a fistful of papers on their desk and offer a grim commentary on all the heinous crimes we inflicted upon each other.

One night I was watching a baseball game that ran well past midnight here in New York. After the game, the station rushed on the 11 O'clock news broadcast like waiters delivering steaming hot plates to a table with their bare hands. The reporters were talking with such urgency and dread, you would have thought the president was just assassinated or a report just as pressing. Yet the only "news" they had to offer us viewers was a water pipe bursting in uptown Manhattan that was flooding the street.

I find it hard to believe that anyone who had stayed up late to watch the end of the ball game really cared about anything more than simply going to bed or doing more of what they were already doing—maybe drinking beer or smoking crack. And I'm positive that not ONE person cared that a water pipe burst uptown—certainly not anyone on Long Island or New Jersey. Yet the newscasters spoke like we were all going to die because of this burst pipe, and they were honored to be delivering this grave information to us before we stepped outside and were swept away by the tidal wave.

Everyone from a toddler to a 90 year-old has a cell phone with web access and if they REALLY needed to be informed of the world's events, they could have been doing that while the baseball game was on. Personally, I could have cared less about what was going on in the world. If it was something super important, they would have interrupted the game with a news flash. Otherwise, I'm more than happy to hear about it the next day when I wake up. If it was world-ending information like Armageddon or the plague, I would have slept right through it and died in my sleep anyway.

Who wants to hear about the day's murders and political corruptions right before going to sleep anyway? Do television stations think the 11 O'clock news helps people prepare for a good night's rest? Recapping the day's atrocities? I don't get it. I'm positive I'm not alone on this. I know there are tons of people my age and younger who think the 11 O'clock news is as relevant as looking for something in a phone book. It's totally and completely antiquated.

Many channels now have late night programming in place of the 11 O'clock news. Humorous talk shows are 1,000 times more pleasant than hearing about the day's drunk driving deaths. For some reason certain channels have the 10 O'clock news—for those who need their anxiety-inducing murder count an hour earlier.

A lot of times, the channel you're watching will sneak in a quick 11 O'clock news "Special Report" promo during the telecast to entice you to stay tuned after the program you're watching. They always say "immediately after the game" because they know people don't care and if they let one second of time elapse between the end of the show and the beginning of the newscast, people will flick it off. Usually it's a news story filled with such hyperbole that it's laughable.

"Doing something that might kill you and your family? Find out if you're one of millions doing it, tonight at 11."

Love those quick hit promos! Then you tune in to the news and they tell you something ridiculous like smoking will kill you. Really? No shit? Smoking, huh? THAT's the Special Report?

The news is really easy to follow these days and hardly requires any reading at all. You can hop on CNN or Reddit and find out the world's events in about ten seconds. All you have to do is read the bold headlines in each section or catch a few keywords. If you need more relevant info in your immediate world, like weather, traffic, etc., that can be found on your phone app.

I personally don't watch or read the news if I can

help it. Watching the 11 O'clock news is not news. It's BAD NEWS. That's all it is. Bad news. It's a breakdown of the murders, rapes, assaults and petty crimes and robberies that took place in your area. It's also a recap and general synopsis of local and governmental corruption. THAT'S IT! That's not news! That's telling you how miserable life is and it's a negative interpretation of the world. It's no wonder there's an anti-depressant commercial on every 10 minutes!

It's a proven fact the more you're exposed to negative input, the more your attitude takes a negative outlook. If someone is told that they are stupid or ugly their whole life, they believe it. Why wouldn't they? It's a constant stream of negative input and they don't know the other, more positive outlook on things. Same with the news. If you watch the news all the time, you'd think we live in the most heinous and horrible place in the entire Milky Way. When the opposite is true. We live in a pretty incredible place, in a fascinating time and life is pretty fucking good.

Except when life is kicking you in the crotch.

Yeah, we have problems. Everyone has problems. We lose money, our leaders are stupid and corrupt. There's mass shootings and horrible pollution. There's dangers at every turn. But so what? That's what's fascinating about life. Life is a mystery. The news would have you believe that we should lock ourselves in a closet and not come out till we hop in a casket.

I'm a firm believer in the 'ignorance is bliss' philosophy. The less you know about the world's events, the happier you'll be. Of course, a large portion of our population is just ignorant, which presents a whole host of different and frustrating issues. But to live a longer and more fulfilling life, avoid the constant barrage of depressing information.

Another problem with the news is that everyone believes everything they see on TV and the Internet… no matter how one-sided the reporting is. I have family members recite "something they heard" to me when they're simply rehashing the "bad news" they saw on TV almost word for word. "If we don't stop using plastic cling wrap right now, the world's slug population will be extinct by 2087." Really? Fascinating! And you heard this info where? No, wait! Let me guess. On the news?

The news is controlled by the media with an agenda. They need advertising dollars and they will sell you what you need to be in a constant state of crazy. They'll tell you about every serial killer, then sell you anxiety medicine. They'll tell you about dangerous floods, then sell you house insurance. They'll even tell you about highway accidents in the same breath as a car commercial.

Some news channels are right wing, some are left wing. Instead of fair and balanced, we get leaning. Some have leaned too far. The talking heads are shouting now. Some are screaming. If you've ever watched sports news, those guys are bickering back and forth about any sports related items till they're red in the face. There's more political debating news outlets than ever. You can see what's happening in any country on the planet in real time. All of it on the Internet.

But some governments control the media. They only let you see what they want. Same with the United States. Algorithms figure you out and spoon-feed you what you want.

Who do you believe? Why do you care? Just live a

normal life of moderation and take everything, including the news, good and bad, with a grain of salt. You'll live longer, have a better outlook on things and you'll enjoy life a lot more.

That's good news.

Nut Job

The Lows of Junior High

In junior high school I had an English teacher, whose name escapes me, who would sit at the edge of his desk, cross one leg over the other and stretch it across his body like a 1950s movie vixen extending her gams for a calendar shoot. Then he'd massage the side of his thigh and lower buttocks like a barbecue pitmaster buttering a pork shoulder. He wore these strange Rayon slacks that hugged his skin like sausage casings. They must have been silky smooth to the touch because he rubbed constantly... ruminating... spellbinding us with his words as he polished his ass. Like a fireside chat with your gay uncle in his peach-colored pants.

I don't remember anything about that class except one precious memory when the teacher went around the room and pointed to each student and challenged them to spell the word *environment* correctly – everyone disappointing him tremendously, his sighs filling the room with warm, tragic air, until he came to *me* who actually spelled it correctly. His burst of patronizing pride sent me into a flight of temporary joy. It was a school highlight that I cling to after all these years. It's important to keep these minor victories available to you when you feel the icy wind of life's cruel defeats breathing down your neck. It's also the reason I've continued to spell the word environment correctly after all these years, even though I have spell check at my fingertips. I also sound out be-a-u-tiful and continue to spell that word correctly too. *Definitely* is another matter. I spell it wrong each time. I spelled it wrong just now.

Junior high was easily one of the most awkward times of my life. If you look at my seventh-grade photo, I resemble a shell-shocked carrier pigeon that lost its way. One day I found a pair of mirrored sunglasses and proceeded to wear them all the time. All day. Every day. Why? God only knows. Probably because I was thought I was cool – and nothing says cool like a 5' 7" 80-pound walking skeleton in mirrored shades.

I took a reading comprehension class that was filled with all the morons of my grade who could not comprehend things... reading or otherwise. One day my teacher, whose name escapes me, took a stand against me and my mirrored eyewear. The petite, grey-haired man crossed his frail arms and stated from the side of his twisted, broken mouth that he wasn't going to speak to me anymore if I continued to wear sunglasses in class. I took that as a challenge, but lasted only two weeks before I gave up that stance. The main reason being there was another kid in the class named Rory and he refused to remove his sunglasses as well. I thought we'd fight the good fight together, but I gave up when I realized Rory had been left back already and was teetering on the edge of making it 3-for-3 in the seventh grade. I distanced myself from him as a "brother in *indoor sunglasses as rebel statement* arms" and returned to normalcy. Rory continued to wear sunglasses throughout the year and honestly, I don't think he's graduated yet.

To solidify that decision, someone stole my sunglasses and I couldn't wear them even if I wanted to, so fate came in the form of some sticky-fingered kid who might also wear sunglasses in class as rebel statement and alienate *his* teachers.

That reading comprehension class was where I was taught what a pawnshop symbol looked like. The teacher gave us a test sheet with random symbols and asked us to identify them. The only symbol I missed was three spheres connected by an arched bar. He told us it was the symbol of a pawnshop. I was incredulous and told him none of us was old enough to know what a pawnshop symbol was. We were 12 and didn't need quick cash for crack cocaine yet; we lived at home with our parents who would provide the money for us should we need it. But he was convinced that the three spheres connected by an arch was a very common symbol and that we should have seen it multiple times in our lives cruising through the ghettos of every major city we visited in our Ford Model T.

Junior high is where I really started to stretch my comedic material. Unfortunately, there were other class clowns and they had material too and there's only so much room on the big stage. My junior high pooled four surrounding elementary schools together. Suddenly, I had 8 or 9 class clowns battling it out for the primetime spotlight. The teachers yanked performers quickly because they can only tolerate so much. So, I took a back seat to some of the more talented performers and stayed in the background as a writer and conceptualist. One of my crowning achievements was a long-form piece of material where I told my social studies teacher, whose name escapes me, that my nickname was Fred. It cracked the class up, but through the year my teacher continued to call me Fred.

This square-jawed teacher had yellow hair, slicked back into curls and I'm sure at one point in his life, wore one of those old-fashioned, one-piece 1930s swimsuits with large horizontal stripes. As the semester was drawing to a close, the teacher and his newly grown moustache began shouting FRED at me like a rabid dog. After I was elbowed by a class-mate to acknowledge him, he gave me a condescending smirk and said "You're name isn't Fred, is it?" I admitted it wasn't. He didn't speak to me for the rest of the year, which com-pleted my masterwork of comedy, but obviously turned into something much more wonderful.

The only thing I gleaned from that social studies class was the ability to recite all the U.S. Presidents names sequen-tially. There were only two kids in the class who could do it without a slip. Me and a guy named Luke. Unfortunately these days, I get stumped after John Adams, who was our sec-ond President. I try and do them in order now and I invari-ably start shouting anyone with a powdered wig that comes to mind – usually men who were *not* the president like Alexan-der Hamilton, or someone who was president 150 years after John Adams. I challenge anyone to name these grim-faced, wild-haired leaders of America based on their photo. You will be disappointed at your ability to identify any of them and quickly realize the occupation of hairdresser was not invented till about 1899.

One of my favorite classes in Junior High was shop class. This is where we hand-crafted wooden items we'd eventually give to our family as Christmas gifts. Things like door signs, napkin holders and note paper rollers you could hang on the wall. Our shop teacher, whose name escapes me, had shaved the tips off of every digit on his hands. Some were buzzed off by band saws -- others ground to nubs from decades working with sandpaper. If you stuck a powered wig on him, he could easily pass for James Madison… our 5th or 6th president.

The main thing I learned in this class, other than properly using a band saw, was to let someone else use the industrial Dremel. About the size of a coffee pot, the Dremel had a spinning knife at the bottom where one could write words into wood or bevel intricate edging into tabletops and plaques. Our teacher could write with the Dremel like he was wielding a ballpoint pen. He wrote the word STUDY in script on my plaque, exposing the creamy wood underneath after I'd cut, sanded and stained it a rich brown color. I gave it to my grandfather as a Christmas gift and he put it on the door of his study where it remained for years. I was very proud.

Across the hall from the shop class was the lunchroom. Lunch was my favorite class after art. Our lunchroom was wall-to-wall windows, one row exposed to a small courtyard so it was a sunny and bright place. For some reason, we had a giant jukebox in the corner and everyone would feed coins into it as we ate. Unfortunately, it was the same three songs played every day because there was some battle going on between certain cliques. The rocker stoner kids played *Purple Haze* by Jimi Hendrix, and that would prompt soulful kids to come up and play *Little Red Corvette* by Prince. This battle continued every day for what seemed like months. Fortunately for me, I'm now a huge fan of Hendrix *and* Prince, so perhaps these battles shaped the foundation of my musical taste.

One of my fondest memories of the lunchroom was when I couldn't eat anything for a month because I had 8 teeth pulled out of my head. I'd been blessed with strong teeth and my baby set wouldn't fall out, so an oral surgeon had to yank them. I remember the day clearly. While administering anesthesia, the surgeon asked me to count backwards from 100 and I reached 89. He said in his 25 years doing the job I had counted the furthest back of any person… adult or child. He said most conk-out by 97, but I made it 8 more. It's an example of my high drug tolerance, something my parents are very proud of. During the procedure, I'd randomly awaken to find the surgeon, whose name escapes me, in various parts of my mouth. He'd cap a tooth with a metal pry-bar contraption and cracked one off like a boat captain might do to a troublesome barnacle. Crack! Each time he yanked, my head jerked to the side with boxing-blow intensity. I believe at one point he jumped up and down on the pry bar like one might do to loosen a car tire's lug nut… eventually snapping every tooth from my tender skull. When I got home that night, I vomited a fountain of blood and passed out on the couch.

The procedure left me with about 10 teeth remaining in my face, forcing me to drink shakes for lunch. I was already rail thin, where missing a meal could send me to the hospital. Not only was my head swollen and battered on a stick-figure body, these were the awkward years in general. Up until that point I'd skated by on cute looks and a modicum of charm. But, I was approaching the teen years. My skin was octopus-slick and I would find out later, bedeviled by Rosacea. Most teens have normal pimples... little red dots that occasionally brew to a head of white. I, on the other hand, would get *huge* welts that would form on my forehead like I'd been knocked in the head by Tom... or his enemy Jerry, with a wooden mallet. These welts would rise so high and at such a cartoonish rate, they should have been accompanied by a slide whistle.

This was truly the eye of the ugly storm. At no point would I be at a lower level in confidence and looks. This is the kind of scene you turn away from -- like a terrible road accident. You catch a glance and look away and hope everything gets better. The dripping, toothy, gangly mess of a human that is sliding all over the place will eventually bubble and form into a more solid humanoid-like creature. But watching the process come together slowly, in photos and in horrific memories, is like watching the exploding Hindenburg blimp footage. It seems to go down in flames forever.

Fortunately, I was able to work out my aggressions in gym. One time we had a new student, whose name escapes me, come in and proceed to beat us all up. He was built like a tank and had the attitude to match. In the locker room, he gave me a death stare and asked me if I was "schizophrenic." I said no, of course, but later that night at the dinner table I asked my mother what schizophrenic meant and she told me. She obviously didn't think that was a very nice thing to say and told me to speak to him about it, which I totally didn't do. In fact the next day, while he was holding court in the locker room, he bet me $10 that I wouldn't draw a beard and moustache across my face with a Sharpie pen. The joke was obviously on him. Being the mental giant I was, I drew it right there in the bathroom mirror and on his word, he handed over the 10 bucks.

That night my father looked at my face and was nonplussed by the whole story. The ink stained my skin for days, but I spent the money on treasured Mad Magazines. I actually still have them in a box in my attic.

Junior high was the first time in my life that I had to change classes. For some reason, I felt an impending sense of doom when the class bells rang. Probably because it was drilled into our heads that being late for class was not acceptable on any level. That 4 minutes was *more* than enough time to jam yourself through a packed hallway, chat with your friends, get to your locker, exchange books, then get to your class on the opposite side of the school. These are special moments of the educational system. Making your kids feel like they're on a timer and could blow at any moment. Step through the threshold a second late and the bomb around your neck could go BOOM. It's a nice primer for the real world, where punch clocks and mid-level managers analyze your timing.

For some reason the combination to my locker was written on my locker door. Someone must have watched me safe-crack it one day and felt it their duty to share it with the world. People would open my locker and toss garbage inside. There was nothing to steal, but one day someone emptied a can of fart spray into the locker, which polluted the thing for the rest of the year. I know that because they also left the can of spray after it was done. Not only did I wear my jacket around all the time, I lugged around every book I had as well. It really helped me build character!

Actually no, it didn't.

What it did though, was force me to make a hard choice… and that choice was to not carry any books at all. I arrived to all my classes with one single notepad and nothing else. I remember reviewing my history notebook fondly at the end of the year. I opened page one and noted the words:

The War of 1812.

There wasn't another note after that. Not one. Nothing. Not one piece of information. Literally not one word at all. The next thing that followed that 1812 notation was a wonderfully rendered image of a battlefield where men with muskets attacked other men with muskets. Men fell to their deaths in billowy clouds of smoke… blood spurting from their guts, while their fellow countrymen leapt over hilly embankments in a vicious attack, while others knelt to help their bleeding, dying, brothers.

After my battlefield phase was a series of cartoon strips based on a character I created called Marmaduke Poopstanker. He was a character I invented that looked a lot like the faceless man you'd see on the door of a men's bathroom, except he was in an army uniform. Marmaduke was a simple, wisecracking private who would raise heck with all sorts of shenanigans at an army outpost, mostly inspired by my favorite show *M*A*S*H*. The only difference between *M*A*S*H* and my comic strip was that mine took place during World War II, where there was PLENTY of time for shenanigans.

One day my parents informed me my history teacher, whose name escapes me, had called and told them that I hadn't done any homework assignments all year. I told them defiantly that we'd not been assigned any. Apparently, the teacher wrote the homework assignments clearly on the chalk board every day and I'd failed to notice as I was hand-drawing detailed images of America's most gruesome battles on lined paper every class. Once I saw the homework, I attacked each assignment with gusto – accompanying as many assignments with detailed images of battle deaths as I could. Even if the homework had nothing to do with battles. If I couldn't hand in quality written homework, then by God, I'd make them vivid with imagery.

Through the daily haze I had one class of visual clarity – a place to focus my artistic expressions and would be most useful in all its incarnations. Art class. That class, led by Ms. Luckenhaus, was so memorable that I actually remembered her name! She was really the only teacher I remember through these disastrous, goofy, awkward years. She was a treasure who introduced me to sketch pads that I took everywhere and drew everything I saw or thought. She was as wacky as they came. A middle-aged hippie chick with long, frizzy, dark hair, "Ms. Lucky" wore flowery clothes and preached Viet Nam era catch phrases like "chill out" "mental peace" "no war" and "freedom." Things we couldn't really relate to because we were privileged, middle-class kids raised in the suburbs whose only real problems were what color Nikes to wear that day.

But, we ate up her attitude with a spoon and fed off her crazy, lilting vibe. One time she invited us to her house to hang out and eat snacks and drink soda and I'm pretty sure someone got into her pot stash. People joked that she had a crush on me, as I was her favorite student. Fortunately, I couldn't begin to comprehend that type of thing as I hadn't discovered half the things my penis could do at that point, and that was after years of playing with it. Ms. Lucky was very affectionate and would hug us and kiss our heads. She was a soulful artist and today, she'd probably be fired for her over-zealous touchy/feely affections.

Somehow I graduated Junior High. I'm not sure how. I believe if you can blink and nod, they send you through. What else were they going to do? Leave us back? There was a slew of 6th graders coming down the pipe and they needed available desks. If vacating a seat was the only criteria I need-ed to graduate, then I achieved that goal spacktacularlly... spectagularlly... with be-a-u-tiful-ness.

My Dinner With Frank

After about five hours of doing cocaine and drinking vodka, Frank turned to me and said: "I want a steak. You wanna steak? Let's go get a steak."

And for some reason I said: "Sure, that sounds like a great idea."

I'm not sure why I thought that was a great idea. Doing cocaine for five hours straight tends to tamp down the hunger a bit. Frank had been doing cocaine for 5 years straight, and when you hit marathon levels of cocaine use, your body acclimates and you function normally again. So Frank was hungry.

Frank looked like David Byrne of the Talking Heads if he was stung in the head by a bee and it swelled a bit. He wore huge, square, steel-framed glasses that hadn't been in fashion since *Saturday Night Fever* was number one at the box office. The thick magnifying glasses narrowed his eyes into beady dots and at certain angles, his eyes disappeared completely.

Frank wasn't exactly my friend; more like an acquaintance. He was also my drug dealer. But we got along well. Most people on drugs do.

So, we hopped in my car and went to The Clubhouse. It was a steak house. That's it – just a steak house. It wasn't a nice steak house, nor was it a terrible steak house. Just a steak house. It said The Clubhouse in red letters on a black sign with the outline of a bull's head. You knew it was a place to get a large cut of meat. It was a joint where a blue collar guy could get a prime steak served on a plate, accompanied by cutlery, and eaten in a room that hadn't changed since Lyndon B. Johnson put his hand on a Bible.

Frank and I blast into the place, pale and sweating, like two caffeinated zombies that hitched a ride from the swamp. It was July and pushing 90 degrees with 100 percent humidity. Most folks were by the seashore, eating light fish entrees and catching cool breezes. Not Frank and I. We were determined to eat warm, dense meat on Jericho Turnpike and wash it down with brown liquors. Even if it killed us.

We asked the host, who was also lucky enough to be our waiter, for a table. The place was half empty because it was Arizona hot and 10pm. He gave us a choice spot by the window, which was ideal because it was movie theater dark.

"I'm Teddy and I'll be your waiter for the evening." He hissed.

"Thanks Teddy. I'm Frank and this is A.J."

Most waiters don't want to know your name and Teddy was no exception. He raised his eyebrows, plopped giant faux red-leather menus on our laps and spun away. He knew exactly what Frank and I were all about in two seconds. He had eyes.

Teddy missed his calling as a man who would perpetually star in Village People videos. His blond moustache and blow-dryer hair parted perfectly down the middle gave us the impression he peaked in 1979 and couldn't move on. It didn't help that his tux had velvet lapels and his bow tie was the size of a vampire bat.

"Can I get you something from the bar?" Teddy asked, returning like magic.

"Give us two scotches and I'll have a vodka on the rocks. Make it a gimlet. You know what a gimlet is?

The question nearly laid Teddy to waste.

"Of course." He snapped.

"I'll have a gimlet." Frank looked at me. "You want a beer?

"Sure, I'll have a beer." I said.

Teddy raised a single brow and looked us over.

"So that's two scotches and a Vodka Gimlet and a beer?"

"That's right." Frank stated, almost offended.

"Heineken, Amstel light, or Budweiser?"

"Heineken." I said.

"Make it two." Frank said popping two finger.

And just like that, Frank had proceeded to push the launch button. Teddy did a double take and hung his hip.

"You want five drinks?"

"That's right, jerky."

Then Teddy spun and walked away before Frank

could add another cocktail to the list.

Frank spoke in short, quick clips, and everything slid off the front of his tongue like a zap. This was during the years when *The Jerky Boys* -- New York's crank-call comedy duo, still garnered a laugh. *The Jerky Boys* called everyone on the phone Jerk or Jerky and Frank was destined to call everyone jerky as well. But only the *men*. He called *women* Molly because that was the name of his dead dog and he enjoyed doing Molly, a powerful club drug.

"These menus are huge." Frank said squinting at the choices. "Why are they so big?"

Before I could answer, Frank was asking me what I wanted.

"Filet Mignon with mashed potatoes." I said, thinking it was about the easiest thing to choke down.

"I'm getting the porterhouse for two. What do you think about that, jerky?" and then he laughed and looked at me with two tiny, fiery eyes that revealed he'd crossed over to the dark side. His face was wire tight with the pall of a frog belly. I didn't fare much better.

Teddy placed half the bar on our table and asked if we needed another minute. Frank said yes, even though we'd already decided.

"What is this?" Frank asked confused, raising his drink.

"Your Gimlet." Teddy dripped.

"No, I want that thing with the onions in it. The vodka drink thing."

Teddy shot Frank daggers.

"That's a Gibson, sir."

"Yea, That's what I want. A Gibson. What'd I say Gimlet? I want a Gibson."

Teddy reached for the Gimlet and Frank stopped him.

"That's OK, I'll drink it" and Frank slugged half the drink before Teddy's hand was back at his side.

We drank a few more minutes, and then Frank went to the bathroom. He was there for a while. Teddy came by and looked at me indignantly and placed the Gibson on the table.

"Ready to order?"

"I think I'll wait for Frank."

Teddy slid to another table – one that wasn't bat-shit crazy. Teddy, in his mind, was trying to run a high-class establishment. Sure the place was dated and the customers were lower-middle class, but he was the face of the place. He was playing a part and we'd crumbled that facade in minutes.

Frank returned and slipped me a matchbook with a packet of cocaine inside.

"Here. Hit the bathroom. There's no one in there. Go!"

I bolted out of there and hit the men's room. The orchestral music was piped-in from the lounge and I jammed my car keys into the coke and snorted to the swells of violins. I flushed my bladder and the toilet, and returned to the table. Teddy was waiting for me. It had reached 10:30 and we'd still not ordered and Teddy wasn't having any more shenanigans.

"You ready to order?" Frank shouted.

"Yeah." I said sitting and sniffing. "Filet mignon, medium rare with mashed potatoes."

"I'll have the porter house for two."

Teddy gave Frank another double take and craned his head so hard, I thought his neck would snap.

"Porterhouse for two?" He exhaled and accepted the order. "It comes with four sides."

He held up his pad and clicked his pen with such sarcasm it practically dripped.

"Uhhh…" Frank said scanning the choices… "spinach, onions, mushrooms, potatoes and olives."

Teddy rolled his head and snapped back with a severe eye-lock on Frank.

"Olives isn't a choice, sir."

"Just give me a little cup or something from the bar. Some green ones. With the little red things inside."

"Pimentos." Teddy sneered.

"Pimentos. That's it. I didn't know it was called that." Frank looked at me. "You know it was called that?"

"I think I did, yeah." I said

"That's because you're smart." Frank smirked and turned to Teddy, "He's very smart. And a good artist too. You should see his stuff."

Teddy shot me a complimentary half smile.

"Is that all for now?" Teddy asked disparagingly

"For now." Frank warned.

Teddy stomped away and we continued to drink. We were sweating like boxers and the bags under our eyes were fit to be punched. After we continued to drink and make a few more bathroom trips, our food appeared.

Between the drinks, water glasses and the side dishes, Teddy was forced to leave the serving tray and stand by the table for extra space.

"Two more scotches, my good man!" Frank barked.

"Sure!" Teddy blared like a man who'd given up. "Why not?"

When frank heard the sarcasm in his voice, he ordered another Vodka Gibson.

"And two more beers?" Teddy said pushing the absurdity.

Frank looked at me and pointed. "How many beers do you want?"

"Two." I said.

Two more beers each." Frank demanded.

"Four total?" Teddy said without a hint doubt.

"Absolutely. And a bucket of ice."

Teddy didn't just spin away; he marched. He returned within seconds with a champagne bucket stand filled with ice and slammed it down.

"I'll be right back with your seven drinks."

Frank and I grabbed handfuls of ice and refreshed our drinks. Frank rubbed some ice on his neck. At this point I'd say we were making a scene, but it was well past 11pm and the place had almost cleared out.

By now, the glasses of cold beverages had sweated into the white tablecloth till it was a puddle. Between our cocaine sheen and our dripping wet table, we looked as though we'd just exited the pool. Teddy splashed our drinks down on the soaked table.

Frank hadn't touched his food and was two-fisting a vodka and scotch. Teddy left for a few minutes and retuned to see how our train was wrecking.

"Everything all right?" He said with over-affection.

"Can you bring me a loaf of bread? Like the bread you put on the table but not cut up in slices. The whole thing."

Teddy folded his arms. He'd been riding the crazy train all night, but now he was stonewalling.

"And why is that, sir?"

"I'm going to make a steak sandwich."

Teddy shifted his weight.

"Oh, no you're not." He stated quite defiantly.

"Yes I am." Frank said calmly. "You want to know why?"

"Why is that?"

"Because this is America, that's why." And with that, he drained his Gibson in one gulp and looked at Teddy with blank eyes.

Challenge a man and his etiquette and you may pass unscathed. Challenge a man and his glutinous American patriotism and you better prepare for war.

Teddy threw his hands up and left while Frank removed the last bits of steak off the T bone.

"I'm not even that hungry. You hungry?"

"Not really." I admitted.

Teddy plopped down a huge wooden palette of sourdough bread accompanied by a long bread knife. Teddy, and at this point, another waiter and two busboys had gathered to see the action.

Frank sawed the loaf long-ways and opened the top like a cigar box. He scooped some of the bread out, picked up his plate of porterhouse and scraped the entire thing into the loaf. He tossed in handfuls of onions and mushrooms, and sprinkled olives on the top and closed it. The thing probably weighed about seven pound.

"Hey Teddy. Can you bring me some foil? I'm going to wrap this sucker to go."

Teddy had completely given up. He nodded and turned to me in defeat. "Would you like to take yours to go, sir?" He asked politely.

"Yes, thank you." I said, then drained a scotch and chased it with a sip of the coldest beer on the table.

Teddy returned and handed Frank an industrial-sized foil box. Frank yanked ridiculously long, screeching sheets of wobbly metal and wrapped the sandwich like a metal football.

Frank leaned towards me. "You want anything else there, beef jerky?"

I tightened my lips in a line and shook my head.

"Check please, Garçon!"

Teddy unfolded his arms and slapped the black leather billfold into Frank's hand. Frank mockingly opened the billfold so briefly, it was impossible to see the price. He reached into his pocket, pulled a giant roll of money, peeled off an unspecified amount of $100 bills and snapped them in the fold.

As we stood, Frank handed Teddy the bill and said, "Thanks, Teddy. It's been a real treat!" and we grabbed our food and left.

It took all of Teddy's strength to keep his mouth shut, but he did. I gave Teddy a smile as we walked towards the door, and he flashed a defeated, yet respectful nod in return.

We went back to Frank's apartment and continued to do cocaine and drink vodka until the sun came up. I ate Frank's enormous steak sandwich for breakfast and vowed never to go to a restaurant with him ever again... which was a vow I kept.

Nut Job II

My wife and I decided we were only going to have one kid. That decision came, I believe, while my wife's legs were in stirrups giving birth to that one kid.

Rita's pregnancy went, for all intents and purposes, quite swimmingly. It was all the stuff that happened after which waylaid any plans of a brood of six or seven rugrats. Her body never recovered and it was agreed we'd stick with the one son. Max. He was super healthy, a joy and a total treat. Why screw it up? Knowing my luck, we'd have a kid with three eyes and a gaggle of assistants to help steer his mechanical body so that they could live some semblance of a normal life.

So to complete that decision, we did what every normal couple does after getting married and having a kid… we decide on me having a vasectomy. The big snip. It's not a terrible decision. I was 40 and wasn't planning on having more kids. I wasn't planning on *this* kid! I've been surprised before… at birthday parties and with a fist to the face, but never a child. It's the ultimate curveball, which is a baseball term about a balls coming at you in a strange way. My balls came at someone else in a strange way. I prefer the baseball term 'it came out of left field' but I'm not sure exactly what that means. What's going on in left field? But, if you want to give proper baseball analogies about confusion, it's more like I was the groundskeeper fixing a sprinkler when suddenly I was in the middle of bench clearing brawl… in left field. What the hell is going on around here?

I took a stroll a few blocks from our Upper East Side apartment in Manhattan to the urologist. His name was Wolfenstein or something like that. I checked him out online and he got rave reviews! I believe every man's testicles, prostrate and penis was in excellent hands – so to speak.

When I showed for my appointment, I was greeted warmly by the secretary who was sitting at a table. Almost like a dinner table, with papers strewn about. I'm not sure if she was doing her taxes or organizing files, but it all seemed strange. Dr. Wolfenstein was as polite and caring as can be. He answered all my questions and more. Surprisingly, but also not, was the fact that he did actually kind of looked like a wolf. He had a long, well-groomed beard with a white stripe down the middle and a main of wild hair. He had round spectacles which made me exclaim, "What big eyes you have!" Actually that last part is not true. I wasn't even wearing red. Now that I think about it, he may have looked more like Wolfman Jack, the famous California DJ that was a big hit in the pop culture music scene of the 70s and 80s. At least his beard did. He actually looked like Wolf Blitzer, the calm, well-spoken anchor on CNN. Regardless, this man was a wolf of some sorts.

I believe people's names can reflect their actual looks. I've known people whose last names have been synonymous with their faces. Perhaps that's an Ellis island thing, where immigrants poured into New York from foreign lands, and the check point officers reworked people's complicated last names by either lopping off the back half of the name, or recreating their names based on their looks. I knew a guy named Elephont who looked like an elephant, and girl named Katy who looked like a Katydid (don't ask) and now a doctor named Wolfenstein, who looked like a wolf.

Dr. Wolfenstein explained that we'd be doing the procedure in the office under local anesthesia, which I assumed meant the anesthesia would be provided by a pharmacy around the corner. I never knew what that term meant, but he explained that he'd basically be whipping up some pain-killing potion in a cauldron in the back and sprinkle it over my neither region to numb the pain. Apparently, eye of newt and bat wing are excellent for this sort of task. We solidified an appointment for the vasectomy and that was that. Rita and I discussed the decision at length, but almost a year later, she was still recovering from the birth of Max and it was agreed that we were "one and done."

I walked to my appointment alone while Rita watched over Max. The doctor assured me the procedure was so simple, I could walk home afterwards without a problem. Maybe even *skip* home if I felt jolly enough. Fortunately, he didn't say the procedure was so simple a child could do it, because I don't think children should be doing surgery of this type.

This time when I entered the office, the secretary was now to the left, and sitting in a booth that was a good foot above my head. Like a judge about to dispense a sentence. I believe they were reorganizing the place. Again, everyone was polite and the office was quiet. Dr. Wolfenstein led me to a room and I laid in a high quality, black leather chair that was sort of like a dental chair but made by Ethan Allen. There was no undressing and wearing a robe with my ass hanging out. I simply dropped my pants and laid on the chair with my ding dong sticking out like a waded ball of clay.

I was nervous, but the good doctor assured me this would be painless and being the good and naïve patient I was, I believed him. He produced a syringe and very gently poked my scrotum and surrounding parts with a needle and injected the anesthesia. Regardless of your pain tolerance, having a needle stabbed into your scrotum and its surrounding area is not very comfortable. I happen to have a very sensitive nether region and the needle felt like a bee sting each time it entered.

Many years before, I had a girl tell me I should get checked for Chlamydia after she'd tested positive, so I went to a clinic for a check-up. Apparently this place was working in the 1800s because their test for Chlamydia was to insert a cotton swab about as far as they could into my urethra until the hairs on my neck stood up and buzzed. It felt like someone fisting a t-shirt into my asshole without any lubrication. So my fears of medical work around the penile area are justified.

Over the years, I've had three instances where I felt blinding pain where I saw stars and thought, on some level, I may die. The earliest was in 4th or 5th grade while playing kickball. David Susskind was up and he had a long leg and could kick the ball a mile. He launched the red ball into the sky and I followed it intently while running it down into the field. Little did I remember that there was a metal soccer post in the field and my face ran into it going full-speed. I rang that bell so freakin' hard, I believe priests in Italy stopped and signed the cross. It was a full-on, crushing head blow across my eye that had me screaming and writhing in pain. My eyes blacked and I had a knot on my head for months.

The second worst pain I've ever felt was during a lacrosse game in 9th grade. For some reason, the coach put me in the game because I was wearing equipment and resembled a person who could possibly play the game of lacrosse. I ran to the sideline to scoop up the ball and an opposing player took his stick and hacked it across my wrist like he was chopping wood. My wrist shattered like dry kindle and the pain ricocheted around my skull. I collected myself and limped to the sideline, but it was excruciating. I wore a cast for two months.

The third worst pain I'd experienced was when I was about 25. I was in a bar and upon existing the men's room, I was greeted by a locomotive of a man who punched me as hard as he could in the middle of my chest, separating a part of my sternum from the costal cartilage ribs. It felt like I got hit with a cannonball and it was such a devastating blow that I fell into a urinal. You know it's bad when you can't avoid falling into one of the most grisly and disgusting places on earth… the men's urinal in a dive bar. Took me about 6 months to fully recover from that hit, where my body cracked and shifted till I was completely healed.

But none of those examples compare to the pain I felt

when Dr. Wolfenstein took a scalpel and cut into my ball sack before the anesthesia had kicked in.

To say I saw stars would be an understatement. More like fireworks. Like the entire Grucci Family Fireworks factory went off in one shot. BOOM! I nearly hit the freakin' roof. I shouted "FUCK" so loud the doctor recoiled in horror. He couldn't believe the anesthesia hadn't kicked in. I suppose I forgot to tell him about my incredible tolerance for drugs as well as my incredible sensitivity to pain. He scrambled like an emergency room intern for the anesthesia syringe as blood ran down across my crotch. He apologized profusely and stabbed my groin area with the needle like the killer in a B-grade horror movie. The pain dissipated quickly but my anxiety rose into my neck. The sudden relief of the pain was enough to give me a shot of euphoria. My head fell back and I breathed a sigh as Dr. Wolfenstein assured me that I would be totally comfortable the rest of the procedure.

He continued, and as he did, he told me he would be cutting "A good length of the vas deferens so there's no way the two ends could connect again."

The reason he'd brought this up because he'd performed a vasectomy on a patient and that guy had recently called to tell him that he got his girlfriend pregnant, which I believe may have upset his wife in the process. Whoops! The good doctor laughed it off as one of those little life blunders like when we break a small clay pot with a cactus in it.

At this point I didn't want anything to do with the procedure. I stared at the ceiling and experienced a series on pulls and jerks. At one point Dr. Wolfenstein yanked a thread up over his head like he was twirling a fork of spaghetti and snipped it with scissors. After a few seconds of pushing and tucking, it was done. I looked down and saw two small slices on both sides of my lower abdomen where the scrotum meets the meat. The right side, where the "incident" occurred was slightly larger, where I may have accidently caused some extra trauma by flailing about.

After that, I checked out and walked back home. It was a long walk. Mostly because my legs were bowed like I'd been breaking wild stallions all morning. It gets tender down there. I assumed everyone could sense what had happened to me by my strange and gentle walking pattern. To overcompensate, I looked around like I was on a leisurely stroll… taking in all the sights of garbage cans and gorgeous fresh baked rolls in the bakery window.

I returned a few days later for a follow up so the doctor could check the stitches. Everything was smooth as silk. After the vasectomy, Dr. Wolfenstein prescribed 10 mild painkillers. This follow up visit, he prescribed a series of 15 masturbation sessions. That's a prescription you don't get very often. Going in for a chest cold or a broken foot doesn't usually call for a hardcore session of jerking off. That's an independent thing you can prescribe for yourself. But if you get a vasectomy, you have to empty the chamber and the doc said 12 was a good number, but recommended 15. It was a tough pill to swallow but I had to do it. My wife helped me a few times, but I had a loaded weapon and until I ran out of bullets, I was on my own. In baseball terms this was probably like batting practice. No game action. Gripping the bat… no glove… working on technique. That sort of thing.

The final rip session was in the doctor's office. They needed a sample to see if I was indeed free and clear. This time, I was assisted by a female nurse. Not physically. She handed me a cup and pointed me to a series of pornographic magazines to choose from and closed the door. There's nothing more awkward than a nurse handing you an empty cup and pornography – knowing that you'll be spanking your monkey with nothing but a cheap door between the two of you. Not only that, she's waiting for it. You get a bit distracted during the process.

The selection of porn was a little dated, but there was a large stack and the variety of choices catered to men of all tastes. I'm not sure who does the porn shopping for the doctor's office, but it's a perk of the job, I'm sure. I don't remember my choice. I felt like if I chose someone completely different looking than my wife it would have been cheating in a weird way.

Jerking off in your house is fine but under the sterile lights of an office you feel like you're in a science experiment. Not only that, you assume everyone in the office can hear you whacking away and that's awkward too. It was all business. You don't lose yourself in the moment of ecstasy and shout a pleasurable moan. You just release and go, which feels like a major bummer. "Well, that was no fun!"

Then, after I hand off the sample, there's microscopes and I assume other more detailed analysis. Maybe an interview process with the semen.

The doctor eventually entered with a pleased smile on his face. I thought maybe he too had milked one out in the adjoining room, but his satisfaction was in knowing that the process was complete and another satisfied customer would be walking away into the sunset – legs bowed and stomping meticulously – like a high noon gun fighter.

Dr. Wolfenstein assured me I was good to go and that Rita and I could screw freely without any cares in the world. Of the many concerns I had going into the process, which most men do when you mess with the plumbing: is will I have any problems getting or maintaining an erection? A very legitimate concern, indeed. Dr. Wolf assured me that there wouldn't be any issues. No ED, no arousal issues. Nothing. He even told me that some men even get *more* aroused, and I just thought that was ridiculous. Not a tale as preposterous as those Weekly World News stories about a woman claiming to have birthed Bigfoot's baby – but pretty preposterous, I thought. Although Bigfoot could theoretically still procreate and I could not, so the preposterous level drops a bit.

It's built into our DNA to be attracted to people who can give you spawn. It's how we base people immediately on looks, height, strength, hip width and all these other random factors. But if someone finds out that you can't knock them up, you drop down on the attraction scale significantly. You get weeded out of the process whether they want a kid or not. I figured I'd give off a vibe or a scent that would kick me out of the gene pool. But, Dr. Wolfenstein was right. The fact that I was a free-swinging dick gave me a confidence and an excitement that wasn't there before. In baseball synonyms this was probably like pitching a no hitter... or getting a home run... or playing a double header. Actually I think a double header is something else.

You know, let's put baseball analogies to the side

right now.

So if you have concerns about the procedure, you have a least one case study that confirms it's a fine experience. Just make sure that the anesthesia is working and all the knives are razor sharp.

But, think of the benefits: you won't knock up your wife or your side chick; you may get more aroused; and you can spend a week or so jerking yourself off before you dive back into action. It's really a win-win situation.

No Class

I went to Syracuse University for Advertising and Marketing Design. When I tell people this, their eyes brighten with electricity and their voices rise a few octaves. They invariably ask me if I went to *Newhouse*, which is a division of the communications program at Syracuse that only allows a certain number of people into the program. It's exclusive. It's prestigious. It's for exclusive, prestigious people who've shown excellence in the field of advertising, journalism and things of that nature.

Once I tell the person that, *NO*, that I was just an "ordinary" art student in the School of Visual Arts, their enthusiasm dims like an oven light. The say things like "oh, well, that's OK" and "I'm sure they had a pretty good visual arts program too." It's the same reaction you get from your distant aunt when you tell her you're still single. "That's ok… you'll meet someone SOME day. Won't you, sweetie?"

If you're like me and many other people, you've probably had a dream where you missed a huge test and you're going to fail and have to stay in High School for another year. Or you missed the final exam in a college course and not only are you going to fail and disappoint the people in your life, you're going to waste valuable time and money doing so. It's an anxiety dream and they seem to occur, at least for me, about once every few years or so. These dreams have the same unavoidable feeling of helplessness; much like the dream where you try and run, but your stupid, heavy, cement legs are dragging you down as a creepy, unknown force is breathing down your neck.

If you've ever seen the comedy classic *Top Secret!* Starring Val Kilmer, there's a great sequence where his character, Nick Rivers is having the very same anxiety dream. He's in "school again" and asks a fellow student where the test is and he's informed that all the tests are over. Nick awakens to find that he's actually hanging in a prison cell being whipped across the back by Nazis. He sighs and says, "Thank God" in relief. This scene is relatable because this actually happened to me. Not the flogged by Nazis part, although I'm sure there are some people who'd find that type of thing very appealing. I'm not one of them, but people have every right to their fetishes.

In my sophomore year at Syracuse, I actually found myself scrambling to find my final exam, where I stopped other people and asked them where the exam was, just like Nick did in the movie.

Being an art student, I had a workload of classes focused mainly around creativity – painting, film, art history and of course, advertising and marketing strategy. But every student in any school is asked to stretch their boundaries a bit and take courses in fields that are related, but won't necessarily be in their field of study. For me it was Sociology.

I remember the first day of class quite vividly. It was held in a large rotunda with endless windows and steep steps and seats that trickled down towards a stage. It's the kind of place you see in the movies, where a cascading bowl of students tower over the teacher who's leading the proceedings on center stage, hammering his fists against a desk and slowly making himself the enemy of every student who's desperate to ace the class. These *bundle of nerves* students will carry piles of books that they read through clouds of cigarettes smoke as they do everything in their powers to please the tyrannical teacher.

Our professor, Mr. Goldschlager, was a wiry, yet confident man, clothed in tweed with a shock of squiggly black hair and round glasses with thick black frames – he looked like someone you might find drinking strong coffee in a dark European city... while it was being bombed.

He entered the class to find the students peppered throughout the large arena. He confidently leaned his hand on a chair and looked over the class. There was no introduction, no opening statement. No hello, and certainly no breakdown.

"Prove to me that this chair exists." He stated.

Everyone shifted in their seats, but not a word was spoken in return. He looked around confused. Perhaps we hadn't had enough coffee or maybe too much champagne the previous night. He made the statement again and a guy way up high said something, which I don't recall. The professor wasn't satisfied with the answer and swung his eyes around the room for a better one. I happened to have a choice spot right in the middle of the room... dead eye-line to the professor's face.

"Go on. Prove to me this chair exists!"

I didn't realize we were in a philosophy class, so being the wiseass realist that I can be sometimes, I said "I could go up there and hit you in the head with it" which elicited a snicker from the class.

I don't remember the exact response, but it was something along the lines of it 'not really proving the chair exists,' and that led to a long, boring conversation that had me checking out after about 10 minutes.

After the class I thought of all kinds of things I could have said to support my case. I could have said "If you sued me for hitting you with the chair, we'd have to talk about the chair in court, thus proving that the chair exists." But this retort came way after the class was over. Like way, *WAY* after the class was over. Like 20 years after the class was over.

I love a good convo about philosophy and human thought patterns. I'm a sucker for existential questions about people or things actually existing. But this professor didn't squeeze those feelings out of me, and I soon found myself wrapped in a cocoon of quilts every Tuesday morning when the class took place.

Fortunately, my roommate Fish would kick my ass out of bed and get me to class. I can usually find inspiration in anything, even if something is having the opposite effect from what it was intended to do, but this Sociology class was actually sucking the life out of me. My classmates must have felt the same because for every question the Professor asked, he was met with the same deafening stonewall response. I actually felt embarrassed for him at times because no one seemed to be responding to him in any way. Perhaps we were all too far away from one another to coagulate into a personal grouping that would inspire open talk and friendship. There was about 50 of us in a place that held what seemed like 500. He could have reeled us in, set a tone. But other than looking professorially, he didn't have much command.

When the spring came and the birds defrosted from their igloos, the semester came to an end and the final exams began. I remember the day of the test. It was a bright and sunny morning. Everyone had their head down, bee-lining to their destinations. I grabbed an early breakfast and for some reason, a Snapple peach iced tea, which I rarely drank in the morning, but for some reason carried it to class that day.

As I stepped into the rotunda, I knew instantly that something was wrong. The class was absolutely packed with people. Full crowd. My class had 50. This room was buzzing with the activity of about 200 -- a real-life chutes and ladders board game with people going up stairs and people coming down. I looked to the stage to see a man who was nothing like my professor. This was a younger, taller and thinner man with sandy hair parted in the middle and back in waves -- like a tennis pro from 1982. His white, button-down shirt was comfortably opened at the collar and he was smiling to the class, tossing out papers like propaganda material.

I stood stunned and realized immediately I'd fucked up. This new professor actually saw me and smiled. He looked around the rotunda, then back to the entrance where I stood. He smiled at me again, but this time his gleaming teeth disappeared and he returned a warm "may I help you" customer service wrinkle. I came down the side steps of the rotunda and onto the stage. He could see the look of terror on my face. In a panic I blurted: "Do you know where the sociology exam is?"

He said "no" and turned to the class and shouted with a big smile "Anyone know where the sociology exam is?!"

The entire room froze and zeroed in on me with the reaction of someone who'd just crapped their pants. "No?" he asked the class rhetorically.

The professor turned immediately back to me and sneered, knowing he wasn't really going to get an answer from this packed house and said "sorry" and continued to dish out test papers like playing cards.

I booked through the building and back across the campus where there was literally not one person to be seen. Not one. Not a student, not a teacher. No one reading a book or lounging on the campus. No one. I was in full melt down mode. "Holy shit did I fuck up!"

I got back to my dorm room in seconds because the only thing I could think to do was knock on the door of the guy who lived across the hall from me – a blond-haired ball of flesh whose name I'd never really bothered to absorb. I knew he was in my class because I saw him in there on the first day. I banged on his door. Fortunately, the little piece of construction paper in the shape of Ohio with his name on it remained from the first day of orientation. I saw his name was Andrew. His roommate answered, rubbing his eyes.

"Is Andrew here?" I asked breathlessly.

"No."

"Do you know where the Sociology exam is?"

"No."

I think that was the extent of that conversation.

I went to my room and picked up the phone. I called… someone. I don't remember who. I believe I thumbed through a campus guide and found human services. I spoke to a woman on the phone who although helpful, spoke to me in a scolding and pedantic manner.

"How do you not know where the test is?"

Before I could answer, I could hear her cup the phone and shout "Hey Janice? You know where Sociology 101 final is being taken?"

Janice replied in a muffled voice and the woman uncapped the phone and mumbled "Janice doesn't know."

"Does anyone know?" I pleaded.

"You should know!" She rifled back.

I heard papers shuffle and the clacking of a computer keyboard. The clacking went on for 3 million years. I checked the clock and it was 9:13. A solid 13 minutes after the start of the test.

"Hold on" she said and placed the phone down.

Again, another 3 million years passed as I heard her and Janice shuffle papers and mumble incoherently. I'm sure it was about how stupid I was and what a complete and total failure I'd be in life. "This kid will be lucky if he can prevent himself from getting crushed in the machinery of a low-level factory job that he barely qualified for."

Eventually I heard an affirmative "OK OK" from the women in the background. One of them snatched the phone.

"Law Building auditorium!" she said like she was reviving a dying patient.

"Thank you!" I shouted and tore out of there, leaving the phone in midair along with a cloud of dust.

I ran across the campus, which again was so empty I thought I was the last human on earth, and arrived at the law building, which looked like a bank on steroids. It was about as intimidating as a cement and brick building can be. I scrambled in and found the auditorium.

The fluorescent, buzzy, neon blue room was the exact opposite of our exalted rotunda. Flat, square and without one window, the place had cattled our class into endless long rows of white Formica that was cold to the touch. I was exhausted by this point and I'd lost my Snapple iced tea in the process. The last thing I needed to do that morning was run wind-sprints across a massive campus, but that's what I did… twice. I burst in to the notice of no one, and sat in an empty seat in the last row, where a test was sitting naked, waiting for me to flip it over and fail it miserably.

And that is exactly what happened. I failed it miserably. I failed the test, I failed the class, and I failed to make a convincing argument as to why I failed this class other than laziness, poor motivation or perhaps the ideal that I'd deserved more fiery engagement from everyone *but* myself.

It's a selfish and stupid thought process. My parents spent money and time to get me to this school and I squandered the opportunity to better myself. It was a mistake I didn't repeat.

But I won't beat myself up about it too much. I did learn a very valuable lesson from the experience, and that lesson is Val Kilmer made some really good movies in the 1980s. Have you ever seen *Real Genius*?

A WILDE RIDE

"I once spent the morning removing a comma and all afternoon putting it back in."
-Oscar Wilde

Oscar, you had it easy. I once spent two months fighting over the wording of a single sentence. Two. Full. Months.

Obviously Oscar's deft little statement is about the writer's process. The process the reader never sees. Not just the writing, but the editing, the architecture... the beats, the cadence. The flow of the words. The prose. All the magic and the tragic that goes on behind the scenes that's never seen once the polished work is presented to the public.

In a book filled with a 100,000 words, one comma can be more torturous to the writer than all the words in the dictionary. It's the little things that nag us to the bone. Climb a mountain to its summit and enjoy the victory that comes with the aches and pains. But get a nagging little pebble in your shoe and the trip stops completely until the pebble is knocked out.

After I finished my book *Buggin' Out* and had it professionally edited, I set it aside to let it breath so I could return to it later and give it a final reading with fresh eyes.

It was the end of October in 2021 and the holiday furnaces were firing up -- ready to go full-steam ahead. I hunkered down with work and prepared to enjoy the ensuing holiday domino fall – disguising myself in ghoulish accoutrements, dribbling gravies on warm fowl – brown paper packages tied up with string.

I planned to pick up my manuscript in the fresh new year of 2022, read it again, and confidently release it into the void of the world like a dove into the clear, blue sky.

Beautiful imagery, I know.

Unfortunately, there was one sentence that I could not get out of my head. It haunted me, kept me awake at night, and had me flopping the bed covers off so I could run to my computer to reread the dreadful statement over and over again.

This passage was at the very beginning of the book, right where I needed to grab the reader by the balls and squeeze -- hold on to them tight -- assure the reader they chose the right book to take home and snuggle up beside the fireplace with a warm cup of bourbon.

So, this sentence had to be right. It had to be tight. It had to grab and it had to be funny or the whole book could go down in flames.

My plan to quietly set the book aside so I could read it fresh in the new year began to dissipate. How can I put something aside when it's not finished?

Thus, the torment began.

I had *Buggin' Out* professionally edited, but the fact is I had it edited by not one editor, but two! My first editor, Jay edited the thing front to back, gave me insights, personal opinions and told me what he liked and didn't. It was tough, but it forced me to rethink passages, clarify ideas, and rewrite parts that were muddy. He was also brutally honest about what he thought was funny and what simply didn't work.

Afterwards, I felt empty inside. That perhaps, maybe, I'd adhered to Jay's thoughts and comments too closely. I mean, he's one person after all – right? So I went to another editor by the name of Odilia. I originally looked at her as an editor before going to Jay, but figured Jay and I were more aligned. Odilia was a humorist and worked with comedy writers, and my book after all, is book of humorous stories. So I fed Odilia a few chapters of my book – the chapters that Jay and I didn't always see eye-to-eye on as far as structure and ideas.

I wanted more Jack Kerouac, and less novel-y

Jay adhered to the literal word where I wanted more of a loose, flowing story that sounded more like stand-up on a stage. That didn't always work. So we met in the middle.

Odilia was more of a philosopher -- her ideas more open-ended and liberal. Her edits and advice more free-flowing. Things Jay didn't like, she loved, so my instincts to let things be as they were became justified.

I read the book again (for the 20th time) and began to see her thoughts and ideas on certain parts as well as Jay's. Sometimes their philosophies aligned… sometimes they were the opposite.

But one thing was clear…

They *both* had a problem with the one sentence that I had been struggling with. The sentence that kept me up at night. Jay told me straight up "remove this." Odilia loved it, but suggested a rewrite that was so different, it didn't sound like my voice at all.

I rewrote the passage about 15 times. Put words in, took words out. I referenced the online thesaurus so many time, they started to advertise on my Facebook page.

The sentence got shorter… it got longer. It became so brief it made no sense, then it got so long it became over-explained, clumsy and poorly written. I put the end of the sentence in the middle, and the beginning of the sentence at the end… and of course, the middle slid to the front.

Then, when I attacked the sentence for the 30th time, I sliced and diced it once more. The end of the sentence was now at the beginning and the beginning at the end. The original sentence was so chopped up, it looked like hamburger.

I was so frustrated, I went back to my first draft and copied and pasted the original sentence back in!

Then I began to edit it *again*!

The end went to the front, the middle to the… you get the point.

Oscar had trouble with *one* comma and I was dealing with four! I took the commas out, put them back in… it was like a square dance. The commas Do-Si-Do-ed and Promenaded in and out. At one point they were all gone, then they all went back in, but at different points. I started having pauses where they weren't needed. I didn't even understand what the sentence meant anymore.

Then, the commas became periods! Now instead of one sentence, I had four little bursts. None of them made sense alone, but read together, of course they made sense.

Then I began to question how people read books.

"They'll read these four sentences together back-to-back, right?" I said to myself. "They won't read this three word sentence, walk away, do laundry, then return and read the next four-word sentence and be confused... right?"

Right?!

The more I read this passage, the less sense it made. It might as well have been written in Latin. Lorem Ipsum.

It's like when you say a word over and over until it just sounds like noise. Like weird. Weird. Weird. Weird. Weird. Weird. Weird. Weird. Weird. Weird. Weird. Weird.

It's called semantic satiation: *a psychological phenomenon in which repetition causes a word or phrase to temporarily lose meaning for the listener, who then perceives the speech as repeated meaningless sounds.*

I read this sentence so many times, it became a cluster of words that made no sense. After a while I glared at it and said to myself. "Who wrote this thing?" Me?

This guy is a hack!

Perhaps it would be best left to an AI program to write this passage, or perhaps, a five year-old. Surely they can do better. What this passage needs is innocence and clarity.

What was I trying to say with these now, *four* little sentences?

When I first wrote it, it was a flash of writing. Funny at first writing... a riff. Now that it was analyzed to death, it wasn't the off-the-cuff glib joke I'd intended it to be. Now it was heavy. Had deep meaning. Mainly because it was an internalized statement about how I was feeling about my writing. Was my glib statement now a window into my soul? Did it need to be deep? How deep? It's a humorous book... not a mission statement.

Was I over analyzing it? Obviously. But the most important question beyond psychological examinations into my persona was "could I ever look at this sentence with fresh eyes again?"

And the answer was no.

So I took it out.

The entire thing. Gone.

And that was that.

I was free!

The freedom I had was so liberating that I almost wept with joy. The weight lifted off me and I was lighter than air. The holidays came and with them... pumpkin pies, Amazon packages and schnitzels with noodles.

I released *Buggin' Out* in January 2022 and it shot straight to the top of the *New York Times Bestseller List*. At least, that's what they told me when I was interviewed about it in the shower days afterwards.

The book went out into the world without that confounding sentence that tortured me and truthfully, it works just fine in its absence.

But here's the thing. I miss that sentence not being there. I have regrets about taking it out. It was actually pretty good. Funny, cheeky and a good primer into my sense of humor. I went back to read it again about eight months after it plagued me and realized something astonishing…

It fucking sucks!

That was it! That was the problem the whole time. It wasn't underwritten… it wasn't overwritten. It didn't have poorly placed commas or too many periods. It didn't matter if the front was in the back, or the middle was at the end.

It just wasn't good.

And the sad part is, it took me the better part of a year to figure it out. All the sleepless nights and head-scratching. The 4:00 a.m. coffees and keyboard clacking was for nothing. At least, that's what it appears to be on paper. Upon reflection, I learned a valuable lesson. Trust your instincts, listen to someone else once in a while and take the time to reflect on things.

Hopefully Oscar figured out what to do with *his* comma. I'm sure he did. He's a household name. A much more successful writer than I am, or will probably ever be.

Oscar probably removed the comma altogether.

A wise decision.

THE MALL

The mall is either the greatest invention in shopping, or the worst. I haven't decided yet.

Apparently this guy Victor Gruen invented the shopping mall, but I find that hard to believe, because the mall, an encapsulated, multi-shop hub is definitely the idea of a villainous hive-mind. There's no question it took a committee of criminals to create an idea as brilliantly stupid as the mall. But if Gruen truly was the mastermind of the mall, we have the Nazis to thank/blame for it. Gruen was an architect who escaped Nazi occupied Austria during World War II, came to America and invented the mall. Thanks/Fuck You, Nazis!

Like Gruen, the Nazis also enjoyed funneling large groups of people into one place, and look how that turned out!

For those of you living in a cave, or perhaps, in a civilized country where Capitalism isn't pounded into the culture like a pile-driver, the mall is a series of boxes that have various specialty items in them. Stores and shops. Not unlike those little cereal packs you get with eight different mini cereal boxes… like Frosted Flakes, Sugar Pops and Rice Krispies. My favorite being Apple Jacks because not only are Apple Jacks delicious, AJ is the acronym and that's always the right way to start the day – disregarding the fact that cereal has no nutritional value whatsoever. Whenever anyone took the box of Apple Jacks before I got to them, it would basically ruin my day, and sometimes my week. The remaining seven cereals were tolerated until we could get a fresh 8-pack.

Like this cereal example, the mall has a store for just about everyone. Sometimes two or three stores are to your liking, and sometimes, all of them have some appeal.

This is the love/hate relationship I have with the mall. I want to buzz around the mall and get what I need, but if I go to the mall with my wife, hours pass and I'm on my second meal of the day in the godforsaken place. The mall is loaded with places for her. I think scientists created some stores with women in mind… maybe some mathematicians too. Maybe Nazi mathematicians. They took the square root of clothing, multiplied it by the amount of accessories you can pair them with, divided it by the mental capacity of their loved ones to tolerate it all, and the sum is The Gap. Divide by 2 and you get Forever 21. Times it by two and you get Banana Republic. Times it by ten you get Bloomingdales, and time it by 100 you get Saks Fifth Avenue.

My wife Rita talks about the clothing she bought at the mall years ago. Like it was a major milestone in our life.

"I'm wearing the jean jacket we bought at the Levi's store when we first met!"

I nod my head, but of course I don't remember. I don't walk down memory lane thinking about the clothing of the past. Sometimes she'll spring a mall pop quiz on me.

"Remember where we bought this bracelet?"

I tell her no because I only have limited capacity for recollection in my head and it's not being used on her wardrobe history. That memory chip is being used for important information: like wondering how Indiana Jones was able to ride on the outside of a Nazi submarine in *Raiders of the Lost Ark*. Maybe Victor Gruen could lend some insight into that.

If my wife and I walk by a men's store, she points and tells me I need new pants. I inform her the pants I'm wearing are fine… they're going on 8 years and still have no holes. She says I need *more* than one pair of pants, which is obviously absurd. Who needs more than one pair of pants? I'll buy new pants when the pair I'm wearing develops holes. The stores she patronizes, the pants already have holes in them. They're shredded like they've gone through the tiger cage at the Bronx Zoo. I go a decade and earn my holes. It's a badge of honor. Sometimes it can take 12, 15 years, but eventually I get those holes. People PAY for holes. It's ridiculous!

To compound the endless racks of clothes and deep aisles of trinkets, there's the terrible salespeople to contend with. Salespeople have been known to blatantly lie about something knowing you won't return it when you realize it's junk. A good chunk of selling is knowing people won't make the trip back because their time is more precious than getting back in the car, complaining, waiting in line, getting the money back, etc…

Like at the giant baby store in my mall. I have a kid and I've been through the whole baby thing, and there's no doubt you don't need half the baby stuff you think you do. Baby showers are wonderful occasions so you don't have to buy a lot of this crap, but walking through the giant baby store and zapping everything with those purchase guns is a slippery slope to go down.

Your baby is basically a blob of flesh for the first six months and does nothing but eat, sleep, poop and cry. So really, all you need is a crib, diapers & ointments, clothing, a carriage/stroller, bottles (or other things in that feeding area i.e. breast pump) and things like a thermometer and other health monitors. THAT'S IT! The people at the baby store make it seem like your kid will walk out of the house if you don't have every conceivable base covered before it's brought into the world. "Better get three or four different kinds of bottles and nipples. If your baby doesn't like one, he won't eat!" I challenge anyone to try and stop their child from eating when they're hungry. My son would have sucked the flesh off my finger if I'd stuck it in his mouth.

We have four malls in my immediate area and they all have a Macy's. Those are the sadists who have that horrible Thanksgiving Day parade every year. They've designed the store like a maze, using glass cases filled with perfume and creams, so you can't escape once you're inside. It works! You rotate around the place and you see the Channel No. 5 station you've passed 6 times already.

It's like that movie Labyrinth. You go around and around and you see the same creatures over and over... like

Muppets. Some even resemble David Bowie. They pop out and terrify you. I'm talking about the perfume women giving out free samples. They're frightening on multiple levels. First off, they're wearing enough make-up for a circus clown. Secondly, they're WAY too enthusiastic. Third, they've been standing in a cloud of perfume dust for weeks and it gives them this buzzing edge to their personalities—sort of a vapor psychosis.

You can walk by them eight times and they'll say the same thing over and over again, like they've never seen you before.

"Crimson roses by Calvin Klein?"... "Crimson roses by Calvin Klein?"

Like a motion sensor robot. After a while, you actually start to cave because you're having a mix of sympathy and some weird attraction to the scent, which is wafting off them like steam. The thing is, for men, this is kryptonite. But if a woman gets a spritz on her wrist, she'll hold it to your nose and say "Isn't this nice?" Which is code for: "Wouldn't you like to buy this for me?" Those perfume robot women are sneaky good.

Sometimes I'll enter a store and the salesperson is right on top of me asking if I need help and I'm like "NO! Leave me alone." But, ten seconds later when I can't find the thing I want, I turn for help and of course, they've disappeared. They go in the back and take a coffee break that lasts 15 hours.

"She was just freaking here a minute ago" I mutter to myself. Then I ask the new guy... it's obvious he's new because he's 16 and he's growing a bad moustache... so I ask him and he looks around for the girl who just went on a 15-hour coffee break. Probably in Colombia. After he disappears I just leave the store. He'll be gone for 23 hours.

My mall also has a vitamin store and the people who work there have the enthusiasm of a personal trainer. They shout everything at steroid levels and run around the store as an example of a healthy person who's jacked to the gills on vitamins.

"Be super energetic. LIKE ME!"

I used to work in a vitamin store and it was our Prime Directive to HOUND customers. We wanted them to buy two of everything and the most expensive choice if possible. Apparently, all the vitamin shops use this tactic and still do as I'm always hounded by the salesperson in the vitamin shop. Even if I'm just browsing, they'll ask me four times if I need help. And if I DO need help—oh Boy! They act as if I'll DIE if I don't buy what they're selling because they're supplying me actual LIFE!

Most people don't know anything about vitamins. If you go in needing calcium supplements, the salesperson will tell you five other things you need to help the calcium penetrate your blood with the highest impact or you're simply throwing your money down the toilet. If you don't buy it, they'll smile and give you a passive aggressive, "OK, no problem" but they shrug as if to say: "I don't give a shit, go ahead and DIE for all I care!" So if you're going in for a $5 bottle of multi-vitamins, be prepared to drop $100 on stuff that will sit in your kitchen cabinet for three years.

A lot of malls have mall walkers – people who are zipping around like little choo choo trains. They're quick-stepping around the place. You see a pack of 65 year-old ladies chugging towards you as you enter through the sliding doors and you think "Why are these three ladies going outside with no winter jackets on?" But nope, they hang a hard left – like a flock of birds, and chug back into the mall. They've got spandex and comfortable sneakers that didn't cost more than $45 at the shoe warehouse.

Teenagers go to the mall and hang out. They can't go to bars and drink yet, and sometimes the world outside is dark and dangerous - so they go to the mall. Mall security doesn't care. These are future shoppers. Pretty soon they'll have mindless jobs... maybe even jobs at the mall... and eventually spend their hard-earned cash on things like purses and oversized sweatshirts. They'll spend that money at the mall. The mall is like a breeding ground for consumerism. There's a Starbucks and a chocolate shop in the vicinity. Feel yourself losing a step and you can load up on caffeine and empty sugar calories and propel yourself into another bout of wallet-draining shopping.

Many malls have little booth kiosks. Those are the places that sell stuff even more worthless than the stuff in the stores. They can't afford rent with the crap they're hawking, so they have a tiny box in the middle of the throughway. It's unforgiving these kiosks. There's no bathroom or hideaway place. If you need to pick your nose, you must dig in plain sight.

A lot of these kiosks are jewelry booths. There's one

right across from a high-quality chain jewelry store at my mall. I don't think the chain store was happy to see this kiosk suddenly "pop up." Shoppers prefer these little kiosks because the person running it is 19 years-old. There's no pressure. The people at the big jewelry store have the tendency to carefully undermine your taste if you start skimping on the price, and NO ONE likes to have their taste questioned—not even the guy wearing a pink tank-top, black & white checkered pajama bottoms with brown leather cowboy boots. If you're not careful, the best jewelry salesperson can manipulate you into a high-end purchase, just to spite them! The jewelry salespeople have a stone-cold smile/scowl, with eyes squinted just enough to shield you from their vision, as you probably disgust them. They can be flippant and have an air of superiority, so to avoid being around them, avoid jewelry shopping just to browse. Jewelry shopping is something to take seriously and not to kill time. If you want to kill time, go to the electronics store and watch the basketball game on 30 HDTVs simultaneously.

The mattress store at my mall used to be a big kiosk, but they graduated to an actual space. Business was booming. The customers walk in now and see nothing but giant white boxes lying around. Most people go into a mattress store with a budget of $400 and realize they have two mattresses available in the showroom in that price range—and those are one-hour motel quality. Within seconds, they have to think outside the box spring. The salespeople like to hang over you, creepily, while you're lying on the mattress testing it out.

"Comfortable, huh?" They say nodding like a pimp.

They don't have to do much to sell their product. They say:

"Well, you spend half your life on a mattress, so you might as well get the best."

Actually, you spend about 1/3 of your life on a mattress, but they're right. Spine alignment is nothing to skimp on. By the time you're finished, you've dropped two grand on the mattress, box spring, delivery and all the other stuff you forgot to calculate when you walked in the door. Better enjoy the mattress because the only thing you'll be able to afford to do is sleep for the next few months. And if you do more than sleep, be prepared to reference the baby section mentioned in previous paragraphs.

My fancy mall also has stores on the outside of the mall. Perhaps this is a space issue. They wanted to get a store *inside* the mall, but had to settle for *outside* the mall. It's AT-TACHED to the mall, but not in the carefree strolling area. You have to go outside and that sort of defeats the purpose of the hub system. Perhaps the rents are cheaper.

"The pillow store is outside? I guess we're not going there."

The pillow store's impulse buying customer is seriously reduced. No one travels outside for pillows. If pillows are being offered in the warm comfort of the mall's enclosure where music is playing and the smell of coffee is in the air… maybe.

Every mall has a store that makes you wonder how it stays in business. The bathing suit store doesn't flourish in the winter and I'm pretty sure the 8 tee-shirt shops are cancelling each other out. My mall had a Bonsai tree store, which was really cool. For years I gave Bonsai trees as Christmas gifts, but as soon as the Bonsai tree store opened in the mall, I never gave one as a gift again. I saturated my own market. The one person I never bought a tree for was myself and the day I went to buy one, the Bonsai store went belly up.

Christmas at the mall is another kind of Hell. If there's one thing that can drive you to an early grave, it's the whole 'Sitting on Santa's lap' situation. It doesn't matter if you're a parent, photographer, person-wrangler or even a kid – it's a massive, twisted ball of stress. Crying, urinating, yelling – and that's the parents! The kids are even worse! Walk by the crush of humans waiting for Santa and the second-hand anxiety is palpable.

I watch as a young couple is scooping their three kids, all under the age of five, into Santa's Den of Iniquity and I need a stiff cocktail. The father is aging by the minute. You can see his odometer spinning and his hair graying before our eyes. Mom is in a $500 sweater and looking fabulous – somehow, keeping it all together, but for the grace of God, she's going to get this motherfucking photo taken and have it on the mantle – or else! The kids have no clue what's going on and are trying to make a prison break. They're working together. One goes left the other goes right. It's a nightmare. I thank the universe my kid is 13. He aged out of the madness. Now the only time I'll visit the mall Santa is when I'm drunk and want to get a photo with my drunken friends.

Being a mall Santa is actually a pretty cushy job.

They're well paid. These men are being paid not only to sit and take pictures with babies, but reaping the benefits of sitting on their fat asses at home all year long, drinking beer and never shaving their faces. They're elderly and now becoming morbidly obese has finally benefitted them. I'm planning on this kind of semi-retirement job in the future if my heart doesn't rupture from all the fatty foods I'm swallowing.

The people who work at the Santa photo table are machines. They're punching people through like human cattle. "Come here – go – turn – sit – tell Santa what you want – come this way – what package do you want? – press this button – that's $185." The photo package people are sneaky pushy salespeople. They'll convince you that you need a Santa photo for every member of your family. For some reason, they have photo packages with 18 wallet-sized photos. Nobody carries wallet photos anymore! Who are these people? They also have the photo package that seems expensive for the three photos they're giving you, but for $5 more, they'll give you 25 more photos... all of which will sit in a drawer and never see the light of day. The extra photos seem like a good deal when you're on line and the family of seven kids behind you are screaming down your neck, but once you get home, you realize there aren't enough members in your family to give these photos to.

Christmastime is actually my favorite time of the year at the mall because I go alone. My wife wants to come, but I make it clear that this is a solo run... a one-man job. I'm buying her gifts. She's not allowed to see them. That's not how Christmas gift giving works! At the mall I take one long, twisty stroll through the place, buy all the stuff I need,

and then I'm out. I'll eat ONE meal, probably drink a beer...
maybe two... not more than three or I buy dumb shit. Then
I'm done. If I drink too much and shop, I make questionable
decisions.

"I don't know, I thought a brass urn was kind of cool
for you."

The rest of the shopping will be done online. Shopping online is fun because when a package comes to my door
it's like a little Christmas gift. Even if it's not for me.

"Oohh! Trash bags! Just what I wanted!"

I'm not sure Gruen saw the future potential of the
mall when he made blueprint copies of his first mall layout:
the mall Santas, the kiosks... the expensive car parked in the
middle of the foyer that no one can afford. Did he envision
packs of roaming teens yelling and drinking coffee? Did he
know about food courts and the potential to get any kind of
fast food you wanted in a room filled with mouth-breathing
lunatics sitting on cheap metal chairs? Did he know that fellow architects would design and build structures calculated to
get humans lost and double-back over and over so as to never
leave the place? Did he have a vision of broken escalators,
water fountains, limited benches to sit on, and 30 different
clothing stores all in a row?

We don't have the answers. Perhaps he just wanted a
place to shop so he didn't have to drive all over town to get
what he needed. That place didn't exist, so he created it... with
the other 20 evil humans that he worked with (some of them
potentially Nazis). Gruen laid the foundation for not only the

mall, but for the ultimate shopping structure that would become part of the human experience.

THE MAGIC OF CHRISTMAS

They say it's better to give than to receive, and that goes double at Christmas time. That's the magic of Christmas – the giving. I'm at the age where I don't want anything. I'm happy to not only give gifts, but take the things I own and give them to other people – right off my walls.

"This is a cool poster."

"Take it, it's yours."

"Really?"

"Yeah, Merry Christmas."

"But it's July."

My Uncle Paul is the same way. He has a small forest of guitars and gives them to people like pediatrician lollipops. If you're not careful, you can walk into his apartment for a cup of tea and leave with some kind of Rickenbacker that John Lennon strummed in 1964. It's the gift of music.

But this type of thing happens to most people as they get older. Not the guitar-giving thing, but the not-needing-gifts thing. You reach a point where you can't possibly squeeze another item into your life. Except maybe a new liver, but those are terribly expensive and I don't expect one to be handed to me in a glittery box with bows.

Any gift I receive now is taken with a warped sense of anger because it forces me to fake a smile and find a place to jam it in my heaping piles of crap. Someone gifts me wine or a rugged pair of socks with reinforced toes and I smile like a beauty pageant winner. These intelligent gift-givers warm the cockles of my heart. They have good taste and good sense. If anyone hands me a trinket, it will most likely be at my future garage sale that I plan to have in about a decade. I should probably plan that sale now, because it will be epic. I'll empty my attic and it will be the sale of the century. I'll need to borrow every rummage sale card table in town to fit all the stuff I own. I'll sell everything and make $50 and wonder why I spent 10 days prepping for a garage sale that netted me about 30 cents for every hour of sweat I poured into it.

My father is impossible to shop for. I usually default to historical books about war, which he then recites verbatim at Christmas dinner the following year.

"You know that World War I basically started by accident?"

"Really?"

"Yeah, Because…"

And then we pass the wine around the table and fill our goblets to the brim.

Any gift given to me that I can't eat or drink is basically a waste. Even as a kid I wanted those sausage and cheese gift sets that come on a bed of shredded paper in cheery red boxes. I was a weird kid. Instead of meat, I got Legos, which was great, but to pair the Legos with a smoky cheddar and dried salami would have made my Christmas wishes come true.

Now, I'm the guy who's impossible to shop for. My wife's Christmas list is basically the home page of Bloomingdale's website, and my Christmas list says GLOVES in faint pencil on a sticky note. She goes to the mall and gets me a fabulous button down shirt that I hang honorably next to my Boston College sweatshirt that my niece gave me five years ago that I wear every day. My closet has amazing taste but I'm personally a missed beard trim from resembling a homeless person.

I live vicariously through gift giving now. I get people what I wanted when I was 17.

"Oh look, the Die Hard film box set."

"You're welcome Aunt Ginny."

My son is rounding into a proper nerd at the age of 13. I got him a vintage Godzilla poster for Christmas and his head nearly exploded. Paired with the collectible Godzilla figure, mint in the box with Japanese writing, his other gifts could have been donated to the Salvation Army.

I gift my friends random memoirs about drug addict musicians and tragic movie stars and they nod confused. They don't realize that I plan to borrow the book, and when their memory gets hazy from all the heavy booze and holiday foods, they'll forget I ever borrowed the book. It's a gift for everyone.

I often go Christmas shopping for myself, wrap the item and slide it under the tree. My family scratches their heads and wonder why there's a new gift To: A.J. From: Luke Skywalker. On Christmas morning, everyone gathers around when I tear open my mystery package and reveal a coffee table book on the history of robots in pop culture.

"Wow!" I exclaim, "Just what I wanted... thanks, Luke!"

Even though I don't have much money, I try and give a little when I can. I jam some cash in a card and hand it to the girls at my local deli. It's basically a nice way of saying "Thanks for the 85 egg sandwiches you made me over the year. I appreciate the fact that you smell like bacon every day of your life." Some men find that scent a turn-on. How could they not? But the women at the deli prefer to smell like women and not roasted pig 365 days out of the year. Hopefully they put the money towards perfume.

Working in the many offices of Manhattan over the years, I was always part of a Secret Santa gift exchange. This is usually hit or miss in so many glorious ways. Whenever someone got me as the receiver, they jammed a few bottles of dense German beer into a gift bag on their walk to the office the morning of the exchange. That's smart shopping right there. I would always get someone as my Secret Santa that I disliked in the office... someone I deemed either lazy or inadvertently making my job more difficult by being a clueless moron. I'd be forced to slink around the office and question my workmates to gain insight into this person's hobbies and twisted fetishes.

"You think Agnes likes porn? What about *Die Hard* movies?"

One year I got my Secret Santa – as well as everyone I knew and loved – beef jerky for Christmas. My buddy Ned and I were on a major beef jerky kick, ordering premium beef jerky from a website in Tennessee where you could fill your cart with jerky from around the country. Just about every animal within rifle range was dried into salty, leathery strips for our protein pleasure. Besides the obvious beef, we chewed smoky alligator, snapped into gamey Elk, noshed on spicy wild boar, and even delved into fish and fish skins.

When my Secret Santa at HBO, Eve opened her box of jerky, it unfolded like a movie scene of someone getting shot in slow motion. It took a solid 30 seconds for her to comprehend what she was being gifted. After she parted the red tissue paper and filtered through the brown slab packets and vacuumed sealed sticks donning images of pigs and deer, her face knotted into what I can only describe as... a proper British lady on Safari being handed an elephant heart to bite into after a kill... and accepting it so as not to offend the locals. She thanked me and burst into laughter so as not to cry. Perhaps the red tissue paper was a poor choice as it gave the illusion of digging into a bloody animal sternum to reveal the meaty insides. In hindsight I find it brilliant. This was the reaction of most recipients upon getting my delicious meat packages that Christmas. My father was rendered speechless, which is a hard thing to do, and my grandmother insisted I'd lost my mind, which was true because I'd been eating nothing but salty jerky for months on end.

The embers of my glowing heart were cooled by

these reactions. Not one person could appreciate the beauty of Kangaroo sticks in Korean soy sauce, Spicy Pepper Ostrich, or even the more palatable smoked duck. Sure, their blood pressure may have risen 10 or 15 points, but that's a small price to pay for delicacies of that nature.

Perhaps these were gifts I actually wanted for myself. Like those snuggly-packed Hickory Farms meat boxes I longed for as a kid. But, that's the beauty of being an adult. Once you reach a certain age you can buy this crap for yourself. You'll also be an adult and realize you can't eat a box of dried meat because you'll end up like a hibernating bear on the couch for two days as your body breaks down the meat.... or worse, on the toilet while your body rejects it.

•••

You would think that a fat man that lives at the North Pole and circles the globe in a sled pulled by flying reindeer would be enough magic to dazzle the mind, but apparently not. For some reason, we need to continually add to this magic by introducing more magic. It started in 1939 when the cuddly and endearing mega-corporation Montgomery Ward Department Store asked copywriter Robert May to come up with a promotional gimmick, which birthed unto the world the annoying character *Rudolph the Red-Nosed Reindeer*. They sang songs about Rudolph and praised his glowing red proboscis, which guided Santa around and through earth's difficult weather patterns. I'm sure Rudolph's nose and Amsterdam's red-light district created all sorts of logistical issues that waylaid Santa for hours, killing precious time when he should've been bombing gifts down chimneys under tight time constraints.

Once the Animated Rankin/Bass holiday special hit the airwaves in 1964, it took a quaint, secondary animal character into the stratosphere of popularity. I admit, *Rudolph the Red Nosed Reindeer* is a charming little Christmas special that has enough cuteness to power a 747 airbus around the planet... even if you can see every little dirty fingerprint on the felt puppet faces on our giant, modern HD Televisions. Yukon Cornelius alone has enough charm to carry an off-shoot special or two, and Hermey's pursuit of dental education probably increased dental school enrollment by leaps and bounds.

Every child looked up to see if a red dot might be seen in the darkened December night sky – filling their hearts with wonder. Before Rudolph, catching Santa doing his dirty work or zipping across the sky was a high priority, but suddenly, a reindeer with a red nose took the top spot in the UFO search. Rudolph snatched the thunder from a man who'd put some real time and effort into his notoriety. Working tirelessly 365 days a year, Santa slaved for hundreds of years to supply the world's children with toys – then, Wham! Forgotten like a caboose with square wheels. Every tabletop decoration, framed print, or yellowing postcard made before 1964 depicting Santa and his reindeer sans Rudolph, was met with confusion and disapproval by children far and wide.

"Where's Rudolph?" they'd cry. "How can Santa possibly fly without a proper lighting system to guide his sleigh?"

I admit, I was one of those little brats fascinated by Rudolph. After my 30th inquiry about why Rudolph was missing from some 1945 ornament or statuette, my father basically said:

"Listen, Rudolph is something that came out a few years ago. It's a story. We're not even sure if Rudolph is real. Before the story of Rudolph, it was just Santa and his eight reindeer. That's why all these things have the original Santa."

That was enough to not only shut me up, but snatch a tiny piece of Christmas magic away from my greedy little hands. After that, I looked at these Santa depictions differently. Pre- and Post-Rudolph years. Similar to Europe Pre- and Post-World War II.

Again, a fat guy in a red suit flying the skies in a sled powered by magical flying reindeer, one with a glowing red nose, was not enough magic. Dash 40 years forward and we've added more magic to the holiday season with *Elf on a Shelf*. These spying elves move around at night and cause different levels of mischief. During the day, they watch over us and report any bad behavior to Santa with an itemized list of infractions. Previously it was only Santa that had the magic, but apparently elves have magic too... disregarding the fact that they're elves, a creature that doesn't actually exist in the world. These little elves fly around like Tinker Bell and sprinkle fairy dust and work in close relation with the FBI to monitor our every move.

Of course children think these elves are wonderfully charming. They awaken each day to see the elves involved in a new activity: feeding the cat, knocking bulbs off the tree, or performing strap-on anal sex with one other. We often forget to move the elves and my son wonders what happened;

why didn't they move? We need to explain that they don't move every night... sometimes they're happy where they are. Sometimes they drink too much wine and are too zonked to get up and move their lazy asses.

Eventually *Elf on a Shelf* got an animated special too, filled with cuddly, charming elves and their mission to report all the good and bad to Santa... like a bunch of snitches. Of course, like any good marketing scheme, they introduced a girl, which is EXACTLY like the boy except she has lipstick and long eye lashes. The introduction of a reindeer was expected because we need more reindeer at Christmas. Pretty soon they'll have dream kitchen homes in Malibu and children will grow up disappointed when their dreams of having a house on the beach in Malibu is replaced with a rotting shack in Dayton, Ohio. One thing these shelf-straddling elves don't have is feet. For some reason their legs taper down to nubs like land-mine victims. It's disturbing.

I'm not sure what magical thing they'll introduce next. There's only so much space in the magical Christmas manger. Speaking of the manger, this is supposed to be a holiday celebrating Jesus, a man born to a virgin, inseminated by God. That's pretty magical! The most magical part of the story being Joseph sticking around through all this stuff. He's a better man than I am – and my middle name is Joseph! He pulled a pregnant woman, carrying a baby that wasn't his, through the desert on a donkey, and slept with dirty animals on a pile of hay. I would have checked out of the situation a long time ago and checked into a motel. The nativity scene we own doesn't depict any doctors standing around, so I assume

Joseph did the birthing as well. But I suppose that's the moral of the story. Joey's dedication to Jesus and Mary, and maybe knowing that three kings were going to show up with gold and other gifts – things he could use to get out of debt and maybe buy a small house somewhere.

I've heard Tel Aviv is very nice in December.

•••

Not only am I budget deficient to be a proper Santa, I'm also girth deficient. Regardless of how many creamy nogs, hearty stouts and gravy-covered potatoes I eat, it fails to make a bowl of jelly around my midsection. Not only that, I barely have time to do the things on my personal 'to-do' list, so being Santa with an unruly list of roughly one billion children to gift is way beyond my personal abilities.

Fortunately, we have the Santa's of the world to help us out. In America we have the big man in red who drops down your chimney. If you don't have a chimney, you must invent a way for him to get into your house when a child invariably asks: "What if you don't have a chimney?"

The excuses I've defaulted to range from "He uses magic" to "he has keys to every home!" In my more unprepared, nog-influenced moments, I've blurted out "he opens a window and climbs in" – like a drunk husband home from a late night bender. This appears to be strictly an American problem. Most cultures don't have the American version of Santa where his eight reindeer climb on your poorly engineered roof and access your house via chimney.

In Russia, a demon wizard named Ded Moroz comes

to kidnap naughty children. What this has to do with the magic of Christmas, I have no idea, but he sounds more like an evil character from *The Lord of the Rings* and I believe you can summon him at other times by playing Led Zeppelin's *Stairway to Heaven* backwards on a record player. Either way, it's a warm-hearted tradition in the Slavic regions. Nowadays Ded travels with Snegurochka the Snow Maiden, who gives gifts to the children, but is probably a witch that should be burned at the stake.

In Finland, the holiday tradition is Joulupukki, or Yule Goat – the Finnish Santa. Although not a demon wizard, Yule Goat was a vengeful spirit associated with the Norse god Odin who banged on doors and demanded gifts and food from Yuletide feasts. How this tradition started is unclear, but these days he is more of a giver than a receiver – a relief to paranoid young Finnish children. Like America's Santa, Yule Goat gets around by sleigh but his reindeer don't fly, which makes him an easy target. Modern day celebrations have Yule Goat depictions made of straw and lit on fire, very likely to burn any witches that might be in the immediate area.

In Sweden, Jultomten is a garden gnome known to do the Devil's dirty work and comes in a sleigh pulled by goats and protects farmhouses from bad luck. This tradition seems a little backwards as Satan is usually not a protector of bad things but a purveyor of bad things. But Satan and Santa have very similar spellings and both are red, so perhaps the two icons are not that far apart in nature. Today, Jultomten the gnome gives gifts to kids who are good throughout the year.

In Iceland, they seemed to have combined all of these nutty ideas into one. The 13 Yule Lads are a pack of mischievous elves who play tricks on children. Like Yule Goat, they'll steal your food or get Gryla, their mother to kidnap you if you behave badly. How kidnapping and ransom became joyous traditions in these places is hard to comprehend, but these are lands known to be -50 degrees Celsius in the summer, so the people and their brains are functioning in strange and mysterious ways.

Of course, who are we to judge other Santa cultures? The American Santa is a fat elf who flies on a sled pulled by reindeer. He smokes a pipe while stuffing stockings. That reminds me of a carpenter I used to work with who smoked all day on the job. He basically blinked non-stop because smoke was constantly in his eyes while he nailed things to a wall using a high-powered nail gun that could kill someone if used improperly.

A lot of countries have Santa wearing clothing more in line to be the next Pope. They have golden canes and towering bishop hats… things priests and witch doctors love. The American Santa is based on a monk named St. Nicholas from the year 80 AD, a time when everyone wore robes because fashion hadn't really been invented yet. St. Nick was the patron saint of children and helped the poor.

As the years wore on and storybooks and advertisements depicting Santa became more prominent, he eventually morphed into a chubby, red-suited man. Much of what we honor about Santa comes from Dutch culture. The name Santa Claus derives from the name Sinter Klaas, who I believe was also a character in the film *Die Hard*, the greatest Christmas movie ever made. Yes, Virginia, the best…

In Italy, instead of Santa, a good-natured witch named

La Befana flies around on a broomstick and gifts toys to children. It's obvious the lazy Italians just carried over their Halloween traditions and shoehorned them into Christmas traditions. Speaking of shoehorning, our American Santa Claus gives naughty kids coal in their stocking while the 13 Icelandic Yule Lads jam rotten potatoes into the shoes of naughty children. In France, Père Noël appears in a red cloak and stuffs gifts in kids shoes, but travels with Père Fouettard, a nasty sidekick named "the whipping father" who beats children who've been bad all year. Call me crackers, but I prefer a nice lump of coal over a lump on the head.

In Austria, they like to mix their paganism as much as the next country by parading Krampus around. Krampus, a horned, anthropomorphic satanic goat appears on the same night as St. Nicolas, his supposed twin brother. Again, we have the Satan/Santa thing happening. While St. Nick is a delightful, jolly old elf who bestows gifts to children, Krampus has been known to dish out beatings to children who are bad. The Krampus warns: "do better next year" and if I was viciously beaten by a devilish goat near Christmas, I'd redouble my efforts to clean up my act. I know it's better to give than to receive, but I don't think that appraisal was made with beatings by Satanic sheep in mind. To celebrate the Krampus, people don frightening wooden masks and smear ashes on people who get too close. Obviously this sounds more like a human sacrifice ritual than a Christmas celebration. Toss a pentagram on the floor and this observance could open a portal to hell. For some reason the Austrians felt this was akin to stringing cranberries and popcorn across the fireplace. Austria is also the country where Hitler was born and raised and there's no doubt he was beaten by Krampus in his formative years.

In my wife's home country of Brazil, they have Papai Noel, which is exactly like the American Santa except he comes in through the window (like the drunk husband) as Brazil is a tropical country that doesn't really have chimneys. In England, Santa goes by Father Christmas and is usually draped in green with a ring of ivy over his head – similar to the drunk husband, except he didn't make it through the window and instead slept in the bushes.

Like many countries, children give Santa their desired wish lists and hope they'll be fulfilled.

In Asia, Christmas is a mixed bag. In the Philippines, they straight up celebrate Santa Claus and he comes to bring good cheer. He doesn't always leave gifts, he just shows up waving and is as happy as a fat man can be. Fly the sleigh up a bit to China and Christmas is still a bit of a mystery. The younger Chinese generations celebrate a bit by hanging stockings for Dun Che Lao Ren, the "Christmas Old Man," but the elders find it a confusing ritual. In America, every Chinese restaurant from New York to Los Angeles is packed with Jews on Christmas Day, so perhaps the Chinese don't quite know what to make of Christmas yet. The children in China give apples wrapped in colorful cellophane as gifts, and anyone living in a country where people aren't dying of starvation, an apple is a boring gift, but for China, where anything from a bat to dirt could be on the dinner menu, it brings tremendous joy. Back in ancient England, fruit like oranges were a common gift and were sometimes used as an ornament for the Christmas tree. Considering half the population most likely died from scurvy, a healthy orange packed with vitamin C was considered not only an excellent gift, but basically medicine.

In Korea, Christmas is a fairly new holiday where Santa wears a blue costume. In Japan, Christmas Eve is a romantic holiday for Japanese couples to exchange gifts with each other. They have Santa Kurohsu or Hoteiosho, a Buddhist monk who watches children with eyes in the back of his skull, which conjures not sugar plums dancing, but incredibly creepy imagery in my head. Thailand is almost completely Buddhist, but since they're a country that likes to party, they celebrate Christmas anyway... my kinds of people. You may not catch a glimpse of Santa Claus in Thailand, but you may see dancing elephants – whether you've been drinking heavily or not. Rounding back towards the USA again, the Hawaiians call Santa Claus Kanakaloka. They say Mele Kalikimaka and have been known to decorate a palm tree or two.

The tradition of decorating trees can be traced back to the ancient Egyptians. Because evergreens remain green in the winter months, they were considered special and boughs were used to decorate homes. The early Romans who celebrated Saturnalia, or the Solstice, did the same. Even the murderous Vikings considered the evergreen tree a symbol of everlasting life and decorated accordingly. The 16th century Germans felt the same about these trees so naturally they chopped them down and dragged them into their homes. It's been said that Martin Luther had the brilliant idea to decorate the trees with candles. What better way to celebrate Christmas than stuffing a dry tree into your wooden home and lacing it with flaming sticks?

Eventually the Christmas tree found its way across Europe and into American homes by the early 1800s. Now

Santa stuffs the gifts under the Christmas tree, which is more kindling to start a fire.

They say it's better to give than to receive and that's true. Between the generous tag team of Santa Claus and myself, my son gets about 30 presents. I look forward to the day we eliminate Santa from the equation. One, because it will save me money and; two, because the millisecond my son is done opening his presents, he picks up his phone and plays video games, neglecting everything that is strewn across the floor.

•••

The day after Christmas is the ultimate post-orgasm clarity. The month-long buildup to gifts and merriment ends with a rampage of paper tearing and exhaustion. A joy explosion. You look around on December 26th and the twinkling lights have lost their luster. Nothing says holiday hangover like entering your living room bleary-eyed and nauseous on January 1st and seeing a fully decorated tree in your living room.

"Who the hell is going to clean this thing up?" you think.

And the answer is YOU.

That's when the magic of Christmas is truly over.

There's nothing more depressing than pulling ornaments off a tree under the blanket of frigid gray winter skies.

When the decorations are going up, you're driven by an unknown force of cheer – fueled by goblets of wine and chocolate. Arctic temperatures when the tree is being trimmed are tolerable because it's all about joy… toss more marshmallows into the kettle of cocoa and splash another shot of whisky into a glass. There's no place like home for the holidays. There's a mystical energy to the proceedings. Fa la la la la and all that.

Declutter the house of Santas and reindeer on January 15th and you feel like an idiot. Christmas felt like two months ago and your house still looks like an elf mansion. You look around and all you see is labor-intensive work. You can still down a few goblets of wine, but the ring of the holiday is a distant thud, and you're not in the mood to trudge boxes up into attic storage.

My neighbors kicked their tree to the curb the day after Christmas and although that's a little premature, they've got the right idea. The calendar flipping to the new year is fertile ground for a fresh start. While fireworks burst and champagne pops on New Year's Eve, my house looks like it did the day after Thanksgiving when we immediately started decorating for Christmas – all while still jamming stuffing and turkey down our throats. It's hard to move on in life when an army of nutcrackers stare at you like a firing squad and your throw pillows say Happy Holidays.

The gingerbread house, which was so fresh and charming a month ago, is now a petrified forest. The icicles that hang from the eaves that we created using the piping bag are now lethal weapons – sharper than thorns and will sting us like hornets. The gumdrop hedges we built along the pathway to the door are still an excellent design choice, but it's offset by the candied holly wreath that someone glued to the front using an excessive amount of goopy icing. The roof halves don't match stylistically and the back of the house has been completely neglected – just like a real house in winter. When the house was being constructed, our gung-ho attitude was intercepted by the fact we were about to run out of the provided candy, so we turned to the Halloween candy in the cabinet, which was still abundant because my son trick-or-treated for three hours and there's enough sweets to feed a military base. Red and green hard candies make for festive décor, but the rainbow Skittles are the wrong shade and size and the Kit Kat bars jammed into a snow bank on the side make little to no sense stylistically.

The ramshackle icing house weighs more than a dozen bricks and when I toss it in the trash, it nearly puts a hole in the floor. It could probably withstand a nuclear bomb and won't begin to decay for another five Christmases.

The outdoor decorations come down easy. Going up, there was hours of cursing, but coming down, well, there was still cursing, but it was limited to about 15 minutes. Unlike the indoor decor that needs painstaking placement back alongside other thin-glass trinkets, packed like eggs into their designated slots, I grab the end of an outdoor light string and yank it off the house like Quasimodo's church bell rope. The lights crash down and staples ricochet around the porch like flies in a bouncy house. When the lights went up, there was meticulous measurements and math; the checking of lights and electricity. The equipment was laid out and organized like a surgeon's tools. Coming down, everything's helter-skelter. The lights that were carefully coiled from last year are crumpled like paper balls and tossed in the plastic storage container like a wastebasket. The red bows that donned our candy cane posts are carelessly mixed with green garland and electric cords, creating a seasonal salad that future me will be forced to untangle in 10 months.

Once everything has returned to normal... the plants are pushed into their rightful corners, the table legs are fitted into their proper carpet indents, and the picture frames are leaning on the end tables -- you realize how boring everything is. Hours before, there was cursing about Christmas décor deep into the new year. But now, the twinkling lights that turned your world into a magical wonderland are boxed and gone. The light that currently illuminates the room comes from a fist-sized bulb that spotlight down upon your miserable existence like a prison tower. Nothing brightens the spirits more than hundreds of tiny white lights setting your world aglow. They sparkle and dance and make even the most mundane tasks more enjoyable. No one has ever gotten sentimental staring into the glow of a 60-watt soft white bulb.

But, you can rest assured knowing the glow of the sun will set your heart afire when it returns to the sky in just a few short months.

In the bathroom

I tend to shower at night. I'll shower in the morning too. I'm surprised I haven't dried up and blown away. I always complain that I need to get into the shower, then it takes wild horses to drag me out. In the shower, no one can touch me. I'm famous in there. I'm in a different dimension. In the shower I've been interviewed by Howard Stern, have accepted a knighting from the Queen, been to other countries and discussed important issues on a panel of scientists. Sometimes I daydream so much I shut the water off and I'm still soapy – so I have to start the process all over again. Then, I'm being interviewed by Ronan Farrow and before you know it, my water bill is in the triple digits.

There was a great TV movie when I was kid called *Bad Ronald*. Ron threw a neighbor girl to the ground where she hit her head on a rock and died. So Ron's crazy mom put him in the bathroom under the stairs and sealed the wall shut with wallpaper. Then his mother died and he was alone. New people moved in and he was the "guy living in the walls." For some reason no one in the real estate agency batted an eye when there was one less bathroom in the place, dropping the home's value by thousands of dollars. But, life went on. Ronald terrorized the family's teenage daughter and... well, it's not important.

My point is – I could totally live in the bathroom if I had to. It's got a water source in, and a waste removal source out. It doesn't have a fridge or a stove, but that can be worked out if necessary.

My wife spends hours in the bathroom. Sometimes days – uninterrupted. It's amazing. I sneak in to use the bathroom and the door opens 15 times and she says, "Sorry, just need to grab something." That happens again and again and then I finish using the bathroom and she takes over again. Now that I think about it, *she* should move into the bathroom. I won't wallpaper her in, but we can get her the phone and a TV and any other modern convenience she needs. Maybe a computer.

We have one bathroom in our house and it's painful. Actually we have two, but the one upstairs doesn't function well. The shower is broken and rusting and the sink is the size of Barbie's Dream House sink. And the toilet is older than plumbing itself. So it's not a great bathroom. When I'm in the downstairs bathroom, everyone wants to use it and I can't wait to leave. But when I leave, no one is in there. I got the impression that my family simply wanted to be around me but that can't be true because when I'm doing chores like watering the plants or washing the car, everyone is missing.

I usually get so frustrated by bathroom time, I occupy the upstairs bathroom in defiance. But then I need to come downstairs to shower. Then I'm living in two bathroom worlds and I'm running up and down the stairs like a madman. But I do that anyway because our house is 100 years-old and our closets are tiny, so my dresser is upstairs, but I hang my clothes in my office closet downstairs. Getting ready for work is exhausting. I lose 5 pounds just putting on socks and underwear. I should cancel my gym membership.

Showering is even worse. I shower downstairs, brush my teeth upstairs... I'm up and down the stairs. I start sweating, then I need to take another shower. It's a vicious cycle. Eventually I'm fully back downstairs, standing in front of the mirror with the other two humans in my life. Also my bird.

Our cockatiel Zen comes to the bathroom too. He likes to look at the other bird in the glass dimension. That bird is standing on the head of the other guy who looks just like me. Zen gets mad at that bird and chirps like a hawk, which blows out my eardrums because our bathroom is an echo chamber and about four feet by four feet. Then Zen gets mad and flies away. Then he'll come back to see if the other bird left. But he's still there! Then he chirps again and sometimes poops. Then I need to shower because I have bird poo in my hair.

To curb the craziness, we clip Zen's wings, but then Zen flutters in like a broken kite on a Kamikaze mission and cracks me on the side of the head, lands on the floor and looks up at me with his little black eyes that say: "Why can't I fly? I could fly yesterday." Then I scoop him up and take him to his cage where he continues to be confused for another 10 minutes until his next crash landing.

Lots of people like to be in the bathroom. It's my dream to have three bathrooms for all the members of my family. Maybe a tiny one for Zen as well. He can look in the mirror at the other bird all he wants. But for now, we have one lousy bathroom.

My wife looks stunning all the time. She takes care of herself. She's got waxes, and creams and sauces and butters. Things that go under the eyes, over the eyes... inside the eyes. Wrinkle creams, anti-aging creams. Hydration gels and collagen fillers. I hop in the shower and scrub my body from head to toe with one bottle of soapy stuff regardless of what it is. It could be foot fertilizer, but I'm washing my face with it. I need that time to talk to George Clooney about my new book and when he and I can cruise around Lake Cuomo the next time I'm in Italy. I can't do that and exfoliate with 9 different shower gels. I'm not that talented.

My wife has me on a routine now, which means more time in the bathroom. We go to the pharmacy and she hands me a miniscule little jar that's glowing blue and she says "use this on your face every night" and I say OK. It costs $50 and looks like it should be holding a diamond ring. I believe it's made from human gallbladder secretions. I can't explain the cost. Scientists created this shit in a lab. They probably wanted to make a cure for cancer, but they realized it was excellent for moisturizing a man's face and stuck it on a shelf. Now it's in my bathroom and I put it on after my 30-minute shower. I look fantastic. Years younger. Like George Clooney. People have mistaken me for a man of 48, but I'm 51, so the money is worth it.

Some people like to sing in the shower but I can't

sing so I beatbox. I'm pretty good. I could probably enter a competition, but I'm too afraid. I've come in first place in the beatbox competition in my head… second and third place as well. But in the real world I'm a no show. I beatbox and get a nice flow going and then my wife's arm shoots in through the shower curtain and points at a pink bottle and says "use this on your face." I pick up the bottle and it says Anti-Acne formula on it. I say "I don't have acne" and she's like "exactly." So it's anti-anti-acne formula. Pre-maybe acne formula? I don't know. I use it. Sometimes I'll use an exfoliation cream and then the anti-acne cream, then some other wash cream, and my face is tingling. I believe that's a result of some of the stimulating wash ingredients, but also because I took four layers of skin off my face. I look like someone that just exited a Navy G-Force simulator where they spin you around until your face is flapping around like a trash bag in a windstorm.

Our towel rack is too small for three towels so my towel hangs over the shower curtain. I'm the last to shower and half my towel is soaked from the other showers. I pat myself down and let myself air dry with the help of our wheezing ceiling/light fan. I don't believe it exhausts anywhere because I've seen the side of the house and the top of our roof and there's no vent. I believe the moisture is going right into the centuries-old wood in the walls. It's rotting from black mold and teetering on the brink of crumbling. The only thing holding the house together is paint.

I sit on the couch and my wife inspects me. She notes that my back is dry and I have to go back to the bathroom and use the skin lotion. I'm very well taken care of. So is my son. Rita keeps us sparkling clean. She keeps the bathroom super clean as well. She announces that she "just cleaned the bathroom." I turn and she resembles someone cooking a batch of crystal meth. She's wearing goggles and masks and is breathing heavily. Her rippling arms are engorged with blood because she's been scraping the floors like a crime scene. When she chirps that she "just cleaned the bathroom" it's more of a warning to NOT foul the bathroom if possible. But it's not possible. My wife has an amazing habit of cleaning the bathroom 10 minutes before I was going to trim my beard and nose hair. I enter and panic because the place is absolutely gleaming. It's like a commercial. Then I grab my trimmer and I panic. Now I trim in the shower. I buzz and trim and do it all in the self-contained area while staring into a tiny mirror. After I'm done I need to inspect the stark white room for evidence of dark-blond face bristles. If one has run free, I must eliminate it. She just cleaned the place!

Unfortunately, no matter how much you clean our bathroom it still looks dirty. It might have something to do with the bargain bin tiles my landlord used that were designed by someone besotted by color blindness and bad taste. Not only that, she hired a handyman to toss them onto the wall like someone dealing playing cards. It's shocking they managed to get them facing shiny side out. Some tiles are facing the wrong direction from the other tiles, driving anyone with obsessive/compulsive disorder over the brink of sanity.

My parents have a nice guest bathroom that is safari themed. It has African animals in sepia tones, fresh-smelling potpourri and little soaps in dishes that resemble candy. Our bathroom is packed with stuff and if you move one nail-clipper, it knocks over a tube of mascara, which acts as a cascading line of dominos until the contents of every shelf is bouncing into the sink with head-rattling clang and rolling behind the sweaty toilet.

Our friends have one of those Japanese toilets where the seat rises when you approach it. It greets you, flushes for you, washes your ass and I believe will do your taxes if you ask it politely. Our toilet was bolted to the floor during the Great Depression and its one benefit is it will survive a hand-grenade blast. Every part of the toilet is a different color as it's been pieced together through time. I defy anyone to get rid of the thing. I'm sure one day someone will renovate the house and they'll spend 2 weeks trying to loosen one of its many rusty nuts. They'll attempt a hand-grenade to dislodge it and it will barely budge. Of course one blast of ass-gas in the bowl will prevent it from functioning correctly and you'll need to call a plumber. I'm sure it's on its sixth generation of plumber by now. They know it by name.

Some people like to read on the toilet. Not me. I like to drop freight and go. I have things to do. But I can understand the allure. Growing up, I had a friend whose father had a magazine rack next to the toilet. Playboy Magazines mostly. Were they jerking off while on the toilet? How does that work? Maybe it was just the articles they were reading. I dated a woman who had a magazine rack in her bathroom. She also liked to get fucked in the ass. Maybe it's related – I don't know. The asshole is right next to the end of the spine. The stimulation is good for the brain. Poop goes out and knowledge goes in. Most people don't like having stuff go into their rectum, but when stuff goes out it's a great joy. The brain is stimulated and creates clarity and understanding. World treaties were probably compromised in the bathroom. I believe the Magna Carta was signed on the toilet.

I remember taking a psychology class in school where the teacher talked about kids who liked to sit on the toilet. Maybe as their brains were developing, the excrement was part of the process. It's scatological. Kids love the word poop. It's fantastic. Everybody poops.

My buddy Kevin was fascinated by people pooping. Not in sexual way, but in a human condition way. He'd ask you how you wiped your ass, what technique you used for the toilet paper (fold or ball) and if you stood up or did the "one cheek sneak." Most people ask you, "where you from?" over cocktails, but Kevin wanted to know what you were thinking while your naked ass was hanging over porcelain.

I had a professor in college who suggested we try and be creative wherever we were in the cafeteria, on the quad or on the toilet. After the 15th time he suggested being creative on the toilet, we just assumed he spent all day on the toilet. That was fine, he had the right to make his work station wherever he deemed fit, but it didn't make us want to handle any of the papers he shuffled in his hands.

It makes you think about others. What are they doing on the toilet? The bathroom is a room like any other room. Some people spend lots of time in there... reading, pooping, scrolling on their phone, jerking off, cleaning themselves, moisturizing and grooming. Shit, world leaders probably solidified major deals in the bathroom. Some directly on the toilet while dropping bait. It's amazing. It's possible huge swathes of oppressed people were liberated while a major world leader dropped a deuce.

Looking in people's medicine cabinets is a window into their soul. Ours is a booby trap and if you're not careful, needles and scissors will fly out like a carnival knife-thrower. The cabinet shelf is about an inch wide and doesn't really hold anything. Once again our landlady skimped on the cost. Home Depot probably paid *her* to take it off their hands. It's so old the mirror is discoloring on the sides like an old photograph. I look in the mirror and I'm suddenly from the 1800s. The lights in the mirror fixture are car high-beam bright. It's a bad combination. Like a fun-house mirror. It's enough to drop your confidence levels or inflict body dysmorphia.

The one saving grace of our bathroom is the showerhead. The water comes out like a fire hose. Crank the knob on high heat and you can feel the skin melting off your bones. It's wonderful. It's why we take such long showers. It's why our water bill is astronomical. My son spends half the day in there. I spend half the night. Mainly because George Clooney likes to keep me at the edge of my seat, telling me about all the crazy practical jokes he's pulled on the sets of his films.

Oh, that George! He's a real yarn spinner.

Nut Job III

I've been to a nut house... excuse me... an institution for the mentally unstable, three times in my life. Fortunately, not as a patient. I may be crazy but I'm not *that* crazy. I've been to the nut hou... psychiatric hospital, only as a guest.

My first visit was an accident. In 1989, while driving my friend Trish to pick up her date with my girlfriend Courtney, we became hopelessly lost and had to stop for directions. Regrettably, we stopped at Pilgrim State Hospital, a psychiatric hospital in Brentwood, Long Island. Why we stopped there, I can't really say. I believe the road signs on the freeway were huge and inviting; and Pilgrims are travelers so it made perfect sense. We hooked a right onto the off-ramp and there we were.

Opened in 1931, the place emanated all the charm and coziness one might expect from a place full of screaming, drooling maniacs. The open, dead-grass fields were littered with imposing, Brutalist brick, castle-like buildings. Inset with endless grey prison windows and towering doors usually accompanied by a moat, the bleak facades assured every visitor they were never going to leave the premises alive. You wouldn't enter the place on a bet, let alone go there on purpose. The only way in was by straightjacket, or one of those Hannibal Lecter hand trucks and matching facemasks. Once they wheel you in to a place like this, you're not sure you're ever getting out.

The compound was without shrubs, bushes or flowers of any kind. I'm sure a drone shot from above would reveal a skull and cross bones. It's the perfect place to film a horror movie except when the Hollywood location scouts arrive, they take one look at the place and leave as fast as their rental car can take them. That kind of horror can't be caught on film. They leave the kind of bleak, skin-crawling terror that Pilgrim State conjures to the special effects crew.

Movies like *One Flew Over The Cuckoo's Nest* depict these places as havens where the goofballs of society funnel in like the wacky personalities of a local bar. The fidgety know-it-all, the cock-eyed drunk… the lovable, off-kilter kook.

Tear away the curtain and you get a real eye for what's happening. These people are locked up for a reason. They're seriously disturbed. Dangerous, even. They're jabbering, grunting, wild-eyed lunatics that are pissing themselves and smashing their heads against the wall. They're not fit for society… and if you've been out in society, that's saying something!

My cousin Jimmy once got tossed in Pilgrim State, but his mania was drug-induced because he'd smoked enough crack to support a Brooklyn cartel. A New York court locked him up with the nut jobs until he could produce some clean urine. Usually when they toss you into a place like that, the first thing you need upon extraction is drugs, but he was forced to avoid drugs.

After Courtney, Trish and I wheeled around the open compound of winding path-like roads, we pulled into a parking lot in my beat-up Jeep Renegade and scanned the place for an entry point. It was agreed that the girls would go off on a mission to ask for directions, and like the sensible person I am, I'd stay with the Jeep so I could crank the ignition for a quick getaway. Like a coward. You could also say I was avoiding confrontation with people who had been partially, or fully lobotomized.

I watched as Trish and Courtney approached a building and were met with a locked main door, so they ventured around the corner – and just like that – they were gone. I drummed the steering wheel nervously until my imagination ran so wild, I was forced to go on a reconnaissance mission to retrieve them. I turned the corner where the girls had trekked and it was a barren and abandoned ghost town. A tumbleweed rolled by if I remember correctly.

I panicked. I quick-stepped it in the opposite direction to see if I could eventually either meet the girls coming around the other side, or at least see a friendly nurse on a cigarette break, or a doctor rushing to a shift.

As I rounded the corner, I saw a large man in a white coat with his back to me, looking down. I assumed, as one might, that it was a doctor looking over some notes.

"Hello!" I shouted and quickly approached him.

As I was about 50 feet away, he turned and I saw it

was a patient in a horizontal striped shirt wearing a doctor's coat. He looked at me with wild eyes – his hands out and clutched, like he was showing me two invisible crystal balls. I stopped, backpedaled with my hand out and said "sorry." The man panicked, his mouth agape and bolted from me as fast as he could – vanishing around the corner of the dull brick building.

At that point I was distraught. I needed to find the girls, but I wasn't rounding *that* corner, so I went back from where I came. The place was completely deserted. Not a soul in site. I got to the Jeep and waited on the hood.

Then, I saw the girls coming at me in what I can only describe as '100-yard dash' levels of speed and intensity.

"Get in the car!" Trish screamed. I scrambled for the driver's side door.

It was a living a nightmare. I clawed at the handle, but it was locked. The keys were in the car. Fortunately it was summer and the window was open. I opened the door from the inside latch, hopped in and pushed the passenger door open so the girls could dive in.

In the distance I could see the patient I encountered in the doctor's coat coming at us, only this time he had blood on top of his head.

"Get the fuck out of here!" Trish shouted in half laugh.

Within seconds I was zooming out of the lot while Courtney fed me directions.

"Back onto Sunken Meadow Parkway and West on Southern State!"

I watched in the rearview as the bleeding patient

stumbled into the parking space we'd just evacuated.

"What the hell happened? Who'd you get directions from?"

The girls shouted their list of adventures simultaneously.

"There was a nurse; These people are crazy; guy bleeding from his head; woman grabbed Courtney…"

The girls screeched and wiggled with an extreme case of the Heebie-jeebies. All I know is that when I saw the patient with the doctor's coat, he was not bloodied, and minutes later, he was. So either he fell or was assaulted by someone during the process.

Even though we escaped, in another time, and perhaps, in another place – and maybe even in the horror movie that would eventually be made based on the macabre setting of the Pilgrim State Hospital, we'd be hacked to pieces by a crazy inmate who wielded a hatchet as easily as one might wield a weed whacker. Somehow we lived to fight another day – to tell the tale of how we went to one of the creepiest places on earth and got away scot-free.

•••

I've never been admitted to a psychological hospital and I hope I never will. In High school I did have some psychological analysis administered by a professional Psychologist. I believe these tests were initiated by my parents, but perhaps the school started the process. Someone along the way said: "This kid *seems* intelligent. He talks lucidly, has a lot of friends and is talented in art. Why is he getting D's across the board?"

For two straight days in the ninth grade, I was locked in a room with a woman named Ms. Murphy who wore a black pantsuit the envy of Hillary Clinton. She was about 30, with long brown hair, pointy features and a very soft voice. The kind of mild-mannered voice they encourage people in the therapeutic arts to use so they don't rile up the sociopaths. The only thing I remember clearly about those two days, besides the room, which had all the comfort and lighting of a Xerox machine, was the endless Rorschach tests.

"What do you see?" Ms. Murphy stated sweetly enough.

"You want me to tell you everything I see?" I asked.

"Anything and everything you see." She confirmed.

I believe she lived to regret that statement, because she must have shown me about 20 Rorschach tests and I proceeded to find at least 50 things in each one. Needle-nose pliers, laughing clown faces, arm-wrestling giants, sunsets, and every winged animal that has flown in the sky since the dawn of time.

I saw faces in everything I looked at regardless of what it was. My grandparents were born during World War I and had twisted, knotted furniture made a hundred years before that. I would see faces in every table leg, ornate mirror and knotted filigree breakfront they owned.

My paternal grandparents had dark, German furniture that was so intricately carved, it looked as though a wizard might appear and cast a spell over it. Their living room was a showcase of swooping, viney hutches; leafy, clanging Cuckoo clocks; and blackened side tables that bulged and gnarled into hypnotizing black forests where Hansel and Gretel vanished on a hike.

I'd see faces all over the place, as well as arms and legs... body parts... outlines of animals... and of course: pixies, bearded trolls, elves and every character in J.R.R. Tolkien's repertoire. I saw the eyes of the world watching me in knotted pines, objects appear through the light of leafy trees, figures on the scratched surfaces of walls, faces in rumpled pillows, and every day items float by in the ever-morphing clouds in the sky.

This gift, or affliction is called PAREIDOLIA. The ability to see faces and people in inanimate things. So, to be asked to find *things* in splotches of gnarled watercolors was a challenge I found enjoyable. Rorschach ink blots, by definition, were a fantasy world to be discovered all on their own.

Developed in 1921 by Swiss psychologist Hermann Rorschach, the inkblot tests were created to identify personality, psychotic and neurological disorders. Basically, they were trying to find out if I was losing my marbles or if I'd already lost them.

Although an outside observer watching a Rorschach test being administered might determine what one says about the *contents* of the inkblot is of crucial importance, it's more about how the test taker projects their thoughts and feelings onto a meaningless image. The test *giver* then determines how the subject organizes their thoughts, what portions of the test they focus on, and if they enjoy maiming and killing strangers they met in a bar.

Results may vary.

By the time Ms. Murphy got to the *colored* Rorschach

tests, she was on the verge of breaking.

"Why do you see that?" She was obligated to say through gritted teeth. Her hand cramping into a claw as she flipped another page on her yellow legal pad.

After a while, I gave up and said no, "I don't see anything else." I could have continued for weeks, but I was not only concerned for her well-being, but for my future. Was I digging myself into a hole at that point? Slowly revealing my serial killer mentality? If a person sees 800 things in 15 Rorschach tests, does that reach the point of insanity on some line graph or pie chart? Is that when the men with straightjackets and long, spurting needles filled with sleepy tonic rush into the room and help out?

I could imagine Ms. Murphy submitting the test results to her superiors.

"Mr. Schmitz saw 300 hundred things on these tests, Ms. Murphy?"

"No, 300 on *one* CARD?"

"300 on one…? For the love of Pete – get the goddamn sedatives!"

I asked Ms. Murphy where she got the Rorschach tests and she told me "from the clinic." They were beautiful -- splotches of yellow and coral red that bled into charcoal grey; lime greens with blobs of burgundy and orange.

She looked at one herself and shrugged. Little did she realize these tests were mashed masterworks. Better than those things you make at the county fair when you squeeze paint on spinning cards that look like tie-die when you're done.

Hermann Rorschach and I share the same birthday, so

perhaps we're cosmically connected to these blemished fold-ups. Science and art are connected in many ways, but I don't believe anyone would mistake Rorschach for an artist even though he spent years perfecting his ink blots, just like no one would mistake me for a scientist even though I spent years in science classes.

I never knew the results of those tests administered by Ms. Murphy. I believe they eliminated insanity, serial killer and psychopath from my profile because two days later, I went back to class and continued to be a D student. No one burst into my class with shackles and dragged me away. I was never left back a grade, and I was certainly not advanced a grade. I was hoping for a gold-stamped certificate that unconditionally stated my genius, but that never materialized either.

•••

During the 16 years I lived in Manhattan, seven of them were spent residing on the Upper East Side – directly on First Avenue – a straight shot north from the famous, and *infamous* Bellevue Hospital.

Although a complete functioning hospital – from Emergency Room services to cardiopulmonary care, the name Bellevue has become so synonymous for its Psychiatric ward that the word Bellevue has become a label. A trademark. An adjective.

The word Bellevue sends shutters up the spine. Any ambulance passenger in New York City, regardless of their condition, would be wise to inquire as to where they were being taken. Manhattan offers so many hospitals, but find yourself bleeding around midtown east and you could be going to Bellevue.

Life can be unpredictable; nevertheless, try and get shot on the west side.

The risk of coming across as less than stable under the care of people in white coats who are rushing you through traffic in a squealing van is far too high. Pain will do terrible things to your personality, but say something stupid and you could be healing in a room whose walls are made of pillows.

Originally opening in 1736 near City Hall, Bellevue's current location on the east side of midtown Manhattan at 28th and First Avenue opened to those suffering and/or dying from Yellow Fever in 1798. The 225 year old building not only looks exactly like an ancient place that held massive amounts of people with scrambled brains, it also resembles something the *Ghostbusters* zapped with their proton packs. Surely two and a quarter centuries of dying, broken souls have left a twisted foundation for the building to rest on. The jagged energy of its current inhabitants only adds to the mania.

Back in the day, an institution was not only a place to stuff the crazy people, it was also used as a place for the exhausted, the downtrodden and for those who just needed to "hit the reset button" on life. Like Club Med for the Cuckoo. Except instead of dipping their toes in turquoise beach water, sighing away the stress, they were ankle deep in urine while someone screams bloody-murder down the cavernous hallway.

According to old hospital logs – more specifically,

the infamous West Virginia Hospital for the Insane between the years of 1864 and1889, people could admit you… or, you could admit yourself, for reasons such as:

Kicked in the head by a horse
Ill treatment by a Husband
Immoral Life
Jealousy and Religion
Laziness
Nymphomania
Severe labor
Over action on the mind
Indigestion
Disappointed love
Bad whiskey
Egotism
Feebleness of intellect
Parents were cousins
Masturbation for 30 years
Snuff eating for two years

And of course, one of nature's cruelest maladies:
Salvation army

Then there were those who were admitted for reasons that may have been harder to properly identify or diagnose like:

Milk fever
Female disease
Congestion of brain
Cerebral softening

Bad company
Exposure & quackery
Imaginary female trouble
Over taxing mental powers.

Spinal irritation
Uterine derangement
Suppression of menses
Venereal excesses

And one of my personal favorites:
Novel reading

Of course Virginia during those years wasn't exactly a tranquil setting for stable living. The place was exploding for four solid years during the American Civil War and a good number of the admittances were people who'd been close to a bomb, lost their children on the battlefield, or lost a body part. War is hell. Its implications can last decades.

The northern states didn't fare much better. Large cities like New York were a hotbed of crazy folks. Instead of being spread out across a large area, they were concentrated into one small island. They too had their fair share of war vets who suffered from PTSD, except they called it 'deranged masturbation' and 'vicious vices.' They all went to Bellevue.

My friend Chris Campion was locked up in Bellevue three times and escaped from there once – a feat he describes in his book *Escape From Bellevue*. Escaping is no simple task. Once you're in Bellevue it's hard to get out. You have to act as normal as possible to sway the staff. It's a delicate dance. When you try and act normal, it simply comes across as contained crazy and makes people nervous. They see through the façade. So you try and balance out the act with a touch of crazy, a bit of clarity and as much indignation as will allow… all in hopes of nailing the combination that sets you free.

The brain is a very sensitive ball of tissue. Because we lack proper nomenclature, we call it grey and white matter. This terminology makes it sound as if the brain landed on earth in a fiery asteroid from space. Like a pulsating ball that a squad of scientists found in a rock that cracked open like a walnut. The brain is a mystery. Usually you can't explore it too deeply until the person using it is dead, and by then, the lights have gone out.

The grey mass has baffled doctors for the better part of forever. But one thing is clear, some people are born with brains that don't function correctly and some break along the way. You and I are not out of the woods yet. A golf ball to the noodle can get it malfunctioning and sometimes it gets that way all by itself. Sometimes the brain just breaks. It's not exactly made of granite. The brain is soft, pliable and can snap like a dry twig. Whether you had a bomb go off next to your bed or you just woke up one day and heard voices whispering to you, the brain can switch to crazy mode – just like that. If that's the case you may find yourself in an institution for the mentally challenged.

It's a known fact when Bellevue's loony bin… excuse me… Comprehensive Psychiatric and Evaluation Program becomes overcrowded, they open the gates and let the overflow bleed into the streets. Because First Avenue's traffic runs one-way uptown, the released patients naturally flow in that direction – like a river current.

I'm not sure what the criteria for release from Bellevue is exactly, but judging from some of the disturbed people I've encountered, I assume if you're not openly holding a sharp weapon, they swing open the doors and let you mingle with the sane citizens of the world.

Every six months or so while running errands in my neighborhood, I'd get an eerie sensation that something was off. I'd look around and notice members of the zombie apocalypse were mingling with the normal, everyday crowd; a woman shuffling aimlessly – shrouded by a mane of long hair; a man arguing with no one to great aplomb – using a mailbox as a pulpit; and a beastly figure exaggeratedly stomping up the sidewalk like a real-life Donkey Kong.

It knocks you off balance. Shakes you to the core.

One sunny Saturday as my wife and I walked home, we approached the corner of 85th and First Avenue and saw a man face down, clawing away on all fours. It was next to an Irish bar called *Ryan's Daughter*, so I assumed he was shit-faced drunk. I was about to ask if he needed help when his face snapped towards us like a horror movie and he growled like a dog. Rita and I recoiled in terror. He arched his back like a cornered cat and clawed at us – accompanied by a scream that nearly sent Rita leaping into my arms like Scooby Doo.

We traversed the situation like two people walking the edge of a skyscraper -- keeping our faces towards the madman, shuffling our feet in a wide box pattern and ready to run. Fortunately he coiled into a ball and whimpered. But the incident shocked us.

Eventually the neighborhood citizens pick up their

phones and complain in a mass wave until Bellevue sweeps the area like dogcatchers, collecting crackpots into paddy wagons. Everything temporarily returns to normal, but it's Manhattan, where nothing ever truly returns to normal in that buzzing hornet's nest of a city.

•••

I've never had the pleasure of going into Bellevue… for injury or for mental health problems. The first time I went *inside* a psychiatric institution was when I was dating Alison and her neighbor Lois got thrown into a private facility in Chelsea.

Lois was about 90 and as feisty and sharp as an old Italian lady could get. She was born and raised in SoHo. Ali would invite Lois over to watch violent movies, which she enjoyed immensely. One day we presented her *The Punisher* starring Thomas Jane and after a scene in which Frank Castle's entire family is savagely murdered, we asked Lois what she thought of the film and she turned to us, eyes welled with tears and whispered "it's beautiful" like she just witnessed wedding vows.

Lois began losing her marbles and she even admitted as much. She knew her faculties were going and warned everyone beforehand. Ali was a great friend to Lois and would keep her eye on her, but she turned her back one day and Lois was gone.

After some detective work, Ali found she'd been tossed in this Chelsea facility. We couldn't figure out how she got there. The most likely culprit was "the system." If you're walking the streets, unable to properly communicate who you are and what you're doing, the police will toss you in the nut house by default. Say something threatening against them or yourself and they toss you in there, whether you're suffering from a minor infliction, or knocking yourself over the head with a clubbed fist. General population should be left for violent criminals... not for those on the psychologically disturbed spectrum.

Many thousands of years ago, the treatment for mental issues was to bore into the head and remove parts of the skull. If you think having mental problems is a burden, try walking around with a hole in the head. This horrible treatment was used for headaches and demon possession as well. If sawing into your skull doesn't *induce* a headache, the drilling pain will surely turn you into a demon and the process will start all over.

In the 1600s, when "doctors" weren't inducing vomiting, they bled people -- a common treatment for every malady -- from hiccups, to fever, to people who jabbered incoherently like they'd been possessed by demons. Demons were a big problem back in the day. It was the only explanation for crazy folks. Unfortunately gods and demons were the answer to just about everything – from the sun rising, to the rain falling, to your cousin Betsy who ate her own hair and spoke in the tongue of another dimension.

In the late 1940s, doctors unscrewed crazy people's skullcaps and tossed away parts of their brains like a chef might toss away chicken gizzards. Considering they knew less about the brain than they do now, it seemed rather illogical to grab a handful of perfectly good brain and discard it without knowing what parts were sane and what part were silly.

Quick lobotomies were performed by taking an ice pick and hammering it into the corner of a person's eyes and scrambling the frontal lobe like eggs.

Now everything is treated with drugs, electric shock treatment and talk therapy – a much more civilized combination than ice picks and sawing into the head and chucking stuff.

Ali and I entered the Chelsea asylum with enough security to protect a bank. It actually looked like a bank, and at one time may have been a bank. This was a few years after 9/11, so everything was on tight watch. I'm not sure who was trying to break *into* the psychiatric ward, but you never know. People are nuts.

Lois was being kept in a secured basement facility. The visitors had free range to roam with the patients, most of who were zonked on enough sedatives to take down a bull elephant.

Lois was sharing a room with three other patients. She looked like a ghost. She couldn't figure out what the hell happened to her and why she was there. Her roommate had stolen her glasses and when we asked a nurse where the glasses went, she couldn't give us an answer. The place wasn't that big. Everyone was in ass-exposing gowns and they couldn't leave the basement. Under those conditions, glasses are hard to hide! Lois's environment became a soundscape of shrieking, mad ravings and threats from mysterious strangers in a blurry environment.

At one point I stood in the common area where families met with their incarcerated loved ones and watched a skinny Asian patient, who couldn't have weighed more that 100 pounds, eat an entire pizza pie by himself. Not only was it a stunning accomplishment, it wasn't his pizza. It was brought by the family of another patient, who watched as he gobbled it down like a zombie.

The second time we visited Lois a few days later, someone stole Lois's teeth and she went from looking like a ghost to an albino turtle. In just a few days the ward had drained every last ounce of sanity from Lois, eventually sending her back home to her SoHo apartment a shell of her former self.

She was dead pretty soon after that.

There's a lesson to be learned in all of this. Leaving your house with clean underwear is the least of your concerns.

Make sure you can speak clearly, know where you are, where you're from, and the phone numbers of loved ones at all times. You may say something stupid and end up in a place with no glasses, teeth or pizza.

•••

My third visit to the funny farm came when my friend Mark was tossed inside a nut house in Harlem, a story I briefly tell in my first book *Buggin' Out*. He called his nurse a Nazi cunt and threatened to kill himself. Again, threatening someone with death, especially yourself, will get you tossed in bedlam faster than you can flutter your lips with your finger.

By the time I came to visit Mark, I was a sanitarium veteran.

And I quote myself: "When I arrived, [Mark] was in a straitjacket, pinned to a hospital bed like Hannibal Lecter. The shades were drawn in glowing slots and the room was so sparse, I thought he'd fallen into an abandoned elevator shaft."

Mark's room, in comparison to the ward's free-roaming area, was a cheery treat. The dark, sterile environment was painted with dark blues, giving it the vibe of an office after hours. In the middle of the giant room was a glowing glass security box, filled with people in white coats who bopped around like fish in a tank. It was a jarring dystopian scene – and I wasn't on heavy medication.

By my third visit, a stop at the pub for a pint of beer was necessary before entrance into the depressing foray. A head full of suds made the glowing security cube stick out like a jukebox in a darkened bar.

Mark was depressed and crippled by MS, but he was far from crazy. In fact his view of the world was sober and keen. But, the unfortunate time spent in that zoo was slowly taking its mental toll and when another patient got the zoomies, smashed into a nurse who knocked Mark to the ground and broke his hip, his health went from bad to terminal.

He was gone shortly after that.

You can be crazy like a fox, but calling someone crazy might be a genuine insult. The world is filled with people who are off-kilter, but not enough to toss them in the nut house and throw away the key.

Keeping your mind sharp is the key to life. Once the lighthouse lamp goes dim, the rough waters send the ships crashing into the shore.

Do puzzles, word games and crafts. Create art and play music. Keep the noodle clear and bright. And whatever you do, don't say you're going to kill someone... especially yourself. You could wind up in the madhouse where they fill you up with anti-cuckoo juice.

And if you do find yourself going mad, try and act as if you're not. It's a delicate balance. Takes years of practice. I've been doing it all my life.